A PARENT'S DEATH

A PARENT'S DEATH

A Biblical and Spiritual Companion

Margaret Nutting Ralph

ROWMAN & LITTLEFIELD
Lanham • Boulder • New York • London

Published by Rowman & Littlefield
A wholly owned subsidiary of The Rowman & Littlefield Publishing
Group, Inc.
4501 Forbes Boulevard, Suite 200, Lanham, Maryland 20706
www.rowman.com

Unit A, Whitacre Mews, 26-34 Stannery Street, London SE11 4AB,
United Kingdom

British Library Cataloguing in Publication Information Available

Library of Congress Cataloging-in-Publication Data
Ralph, Margaret Nutting.
A parent's death : a biblical and spiritual companion / Margaret Nutting Ralph.
pages cm
Includes bibliographical references and index.
ISBN 978-1-4422-4327-9 (cloth : alk. paper) — ISBN 978-1-4422-4328-6 (electronic)
Religious aspects—Christianity. 2. Ralph, Margaret Nutting. 3. Death—Religious as-
pects—Christianity. I. Title.
BV4906.R35 2015
248.8'66—dc23
2014038248

Printed in the United States of America

This book is dedicated to my parents:

Mary Agnes Flannagan Nutting and
Charles Bernard Nutting.

"'For this reason a man shall leave his father and mother and be joined to his wife, and the two shall become one flesh.' So, they are no longer two, but one flesh. Therefore what God has joined together, no human being must separate." (Mark 10:7–9)

CONTENTS

INTRODUCTION:
A PERSONAL WITNESS

My father died over twenty years ago. So, the story you are about to read did not happen recently. However, the whole experience seems recent to me. Why? I'm not really sure. Perhaps it is because I think about, pray for, and pray to my parents so regularly that it seems impossible that I haven't talked with my father face-to-face for twenty years. Perhaps it is because some unusual events occurred surrounding my father's death, not events that I would call *miracles,* but still events that seem to me to have bordered on the supernatural. By that I mean that I cannot explain the events without resorting to attributing them to something beyond what we presently know about the natural order. I now understand why people who have had the privilege of accompanying someone to death's door often talk of a *veil* or of *thin places* between this life and the next. As years have passed, these events have had a rippling effect on my life and in my work.

I have worked in the field of religious education for fifty years, sometimes in catechetical settings (Church settings in which we echo the good news) and sometimes in academic settings (settings in which we not only teach beliefs, but we critically examine the evidence for those beliefs). In both catechetical and academic settings, my area of expertise is the Bible. The goal in my studies has been to understand what the original inspired authors intended to teach their contemporaries. In addition to that goal, but firmly rooted in that knowledge, my goal as a catechist/teacher and author has been to understand, and to help others understand, what the living word of Scripture is teaching us today.

For a number of years I was a Diocesan Director of Evangelization. It was part of my responsibility to serve parish evangelizers. In that capacity I helped parish leaders reflect on their experiences of God acting in their lives and learn how to share those insights with others. As Paul VI says in *Evangelization in the Modern World (Evangelii Nuntiandi)*, "Modern man listens more willingly to witnesses than to teachers, and if he does listen to teachers it is because they are witnesses" (par. 41).

In this book I would like to be a witness to the truths I learned because of the events surrounding my father's death. Initially, I simply found the events remarkable. However, as the years have passed, I have realized that experiencing these events has opened my eyes to see meanings in many biblical passages that I had not seen before, passages such as Paul's admonishing the Corinthians for their divisive behavior at the Lord's supper (1 Cor 11:17–34), the postresurrection appearance stories in which those who know and love Jesus fail to recognize him, and the prologue in John's Gospel in which all of creation is attributed to the Word who became flesh. All in all, the insights have had a theme: The risen Christ has been saying to me, "I don't think you recognized me."

It is my hope and prayer that sharing these experiences will have the same effect on the reader that experiencing them has had on me. After all, God is powerful and present in each of our lives and is inviting each of us to grow in love. What remains to be seen is whether or not we will recognize the presence of the risen Christ in our midst and whether or not we will accept the invitation. When we believe God's self-revelation that God is love, and we accept the invitation to live in that love, we see more and more clearly the absolute importance of breaking down all the walls we have built that separate us, one from another: walls between classes, races, nations, and religions. We begin to understand the unity of all creation and our own role in maintaining that unity.

OVERVIEW OF CHAPTERS

Chapter 1 sets the stage for all that follows. In it I describe the original wall that I believed existed between my father and me: I was being raised Catholic and he was Presbyterian. In addition, I describe a remarkable occurrence that paved the way for my having the privilege of teaching Scripture. This experience persuaded me that God, on occasion, still intervenes in events in powerful ways, a conviction I share with inspired biblical authors. I conclude this chapter by explaining the distinction between events in which we experience firsthand God's power and presence in our lives, and events that we would call *supernatural*. We can know the proximate cause of an event, therefore not claiming that the event is supernatural, and still experience the event as a marvelous occurrence.

Chapters 2 and 3 describe my father's death and funeral. My experience of these events affirmed once more my belief that God intervenes in events. When, on occasion, I have shared what happened with loved ones, colleagues, or students, I have realized that some people are overwhelmed with emotion because my experience reminds them of similar events in their own lives and confirms their interpretation of those events as times when God's power and presence were clearly manifest. On the other hand, some suspect I am exaggerating to make a point. I assure the reader, the accounts of these events are as accurate as I can describe them.

Chapter 4 explores the effect that these overwhelming experiences have had on my understanding of Scripture passages that deal with recognizing the presence of the risen Christ in Christ's disciples, the Church. When one has had the privilege of teaching Scripture for many years, one has some confidence that he or she understands what is being taught. However, gradually, over years,

I have found my perception of a number of passages changing and deepening, especially those passages that deal with recognizing the risen Christ or recognizing the body of Christ, the Church. This chapter ends with a discussion of how both the Gospel According to John and Paul's letters emphasize the absolute priority of the gift of love in the Church and in all that we do.

Chapter 5 returns to a reflection on experience, this time the experience of observing people being the body of Christ for others, and realizing that, on occasion, I, too, have been Christ for others. These experiences revolve around not only my father's death, but my mother's death five years later. Both of my parents had a profound effect on those who came to know them in their last years. In addition, caring for my parents brought a number of people together who would not otherwise have had any contact. Such a setting gave us completely unexpected opportunities to be Christ for each other, both through service and through witness. One of the very important witnesses I was privileged to receive was that of a young woman who had a remarkable experience with her mother after her mother's death. Her experience affirmed her hope in life after death for her loved ones and herself.

Chapter 6 responds to 1 Peter's admonition that we should always be ready to give an explanation for our hope. Since I am a Christian, my hope rests in the good news of Jesus Christ as explained in Scripture as well as in my personal experiences, which confirm that good news. However, not everyone accepts Scripture as revelatory and authoritative. So, before explaining the reasons for my hope, I respond to the question: Why trust Scripture? I then trace the process of coming to a belief in life after death that is present in Scripture. A belief in life after death was not a prevailing belief in the Old Testament. Some Jews did begin to believe in life after death about two hundred years before Jesus. However, a belief in life after death is absolutely core to the New Testament. Of course, this belief rests on Jesus, who died and then rose from the dead.

In addition to a belief in life after death, my hope rests in what the New Testament teaches us about the purposes of suffering.

Not all suffering is the consequence of sin. Suffering has purposes other than punishment. In Chapter 6 we trace the growing understanding about the purposes of suffering in both the Old and New Testaments. To believe that suffering has a purpose, that through suffering God can accomplish something wonderful and new, is a great source of hope for those who are suffering.

Chapter 7 reflects on my expanding understanding of the ramifications of the fact that God is love. In Chapter 4 this expanded view embraced all Christians. In Chapter 7 this expanded view embraces all world religions, all sincere truth seekers, and all of creation. First, I illustrate that both the Old and New Testaments model an expanding understanding of the answer to the question, "Whom does God love?" I believe that we who live in the twenty-first century are called to expand our answer to that question, too, and that Scripture gives us the categories of thought we need to perceive the presence of God in all that God has created. The natural consequence of such a conclusion is that we must treat every person and everything as a gift from a loving God and as beloved by God.

Chapter 8 names the spiritual lessons learned as I understand them some twenty years after the events. Here I return to the mysterious truth that we cannot choose to love and at the same time avoid suffering. There is something about suffering that forms us. Even Jesus is said to have been perfected through suffering (see Heb 2:10). Next I return to the mystery of life after death and describe the experiences of a number of people who believe in life after death not only because of the apostolic witness, but also because of their own encounters with loved ones. I then explore further the idea that we are called to love and forgive. This call has profound ramifications, not just in our relationships with other individual people, but in a global context: our relationships with other classes, other races, other countries, and other world religions. To expand the context even further, I meditate on the mystery of Eucharist as an eschatological meal that takes us out of time and space and unites us with our beloved dead. The chapter ends with some thoughts on the mystery of being loved by a God who created all that exists in love and who is love.

Each chapter ends with a section entitled "Spiritual Lessons Learned/Reflections." In these sections I name what I believe to be spiritual truths, pose some personal reflection questions in relation to those truths, and offer passages from Scripture for further meditation. My goal in writing these sections is to offer some thoughts that the reader might find helpful on the spiritual lessons learned when we suffer the loss of a loved one. However, I do not think of these sections as offering advice to others in grief. To do that seems to me to be presumptuous. People experience grief and handle grief in very individual ways. Rather, these sections simply share thoughts that I found life-giving and helpful with the hope that others might find them helpful, too.

When I offer Scripture passages for meditation, I am using Scripture in a different way than I use Scripture throughout the body of the chapters. In the body of the chapters, when I turn to Scripture, I am usually trying to understand what the original inspired author was teaching. To do that I must put the passage I am trying to understand in the contexts in which it appears in the Bible. These contexts include the literary form the author has chosen to use, the beliefs of the people at the time, and the fact that Scripture offers us a two thousand year process of coming to understand mysterious truths about our relationship with God, about the purpose of life, and about our destinies. When we read biblical passages in context, we discover universal truths that every generation needs to hear. In case the reader is unfamiliar with the contextualist approach to Scripture, I have written a more detailed explanation of this method of interpretation that appears as Appendix 1 in this book.

When I offer a Scripture passage for personal meditation, I am taking the passage out of its biblical context and using it to help the reader hear Scripture as a living word that can cut to the marrow of the bone. As Hebrews tells us: "Indeed, the word of God is living and effective, sharper than any two-edged sword, penetrating even between soul and spirit, joints and marrow, and able to discern reflections and thoughts of the heart" (Heb 4:12). The meaning we hear when we listen to Scripture as a living word may not be a universal truth, but may, nevertheless, offer us wisdom and guidance in the context of our own lives. In case the reader is unfamiliar with hearing Scripture as a living word, I have written a more detailed explanation of this method of interpretation that appears as Appendix 2 in this book.

Both uses of Scripture are essential. On the one hand, we want to understand what the original inspired authors are teaching us. We put the authority of Scripture behind the revealed truths that the authors intended to teach. On the other hand, we don't want Scripture to be merely a historical word to previous generations. We want it to be a living word that nourishes and guides us.

As an example, I offer the following passage for reflection, given the topic of this book:

> For the Lord comforts his people
> and shows mercy to his afflicted. (Is 49:13b)

In its original context, this passage was assuring the Israelites that God is their God and they are God's people. Notice the use of the possessive. The passage does not say that the Lord comforts **the** people; it says, the Lord comforts **his** own people. This central belief, the Israelites' belief in their covenant relationship with their God, was core to their self-understanding. At the time of this prophecy, this belief had been challenged by the events leading up to the Babylonian exile. As part of their covenant relationship with God, the Israelites believed that God had promised them a king and a nation. Now, that nation was no more and the king was in exile. What was the meaning of these terrible events? Was God still their God? Were they still God's people?

The prophet's answer to their heartfelt cry was, "Yes." God is still their God. They are still God's people. The Lord is with them and will comfort them.

However, as a living word, the passage can also be understood to speak to each of us who is suffering from the death of a loved one. These inspired, living words encourage us to turn to God in our grief because the Lord is present and will comfort us in our time of need.

The Lord has many ways to comfort us: through Scripture, through prayer, through other people, through reading, through nature, through totally unexpected and unexplainable moments of grace and insight. When we are in grief, we need the wisdom of many others with many different points of view and, therefore, many different insights. In hopes of responding further to those in grief and to those who are accompanying those in grief, I have included a bibliography of books that have been recommended by hospice workers and by students I have known at Lexington Theological Seminary who have become chaplains. While the authors of these books may not always have found hope and comfort in the same way that I, as a Christian, have, they nevertheless have the wisdom that comes from study and from honest reflection on experience to offer each one of us. It is my hope and prayer that their reflections, as well as mine, will be helpful to others.

1

SETTING THE STAGE

Before describing the events surrounding my father's death, I would like to set the stage by explaining a little about my background. In hindsight, I realize that two factors played a primary role, although a background role, in priming the pump for the profound effect that the unusual events that occurred around my father's death have had on my life over the past twenty years.

The first factor is that as a young Roman Catholic I was taught and firmly believed that my wonderful Presbyterian father could not get to heaven. I outgrew that belief, but the very fact that I had believed something that I later rejected as false taught me to be open to new understandings in other areas of my beliefs as well.

The second factor is that my life's work as a teacher of Scripture became possible for me in a way that I experienced as miraculous. Because of this experience, I had come to believe that God had been present and had acted powerfully in my life through events. I remained open to the possibility that such a thing could happen again. In hindsight I think that each of these mental/spiritual postures *tilled the soil*, preparing me to experience the events that were to follow as I have experienced them.

OUTGROWING A CHILDHOOD BELIEF

As I imagine is true for all children, I was unaware that there was anything unusual in my home life. It all seemed perfectly normal to me. However, in hindsight I realize that my circumstances were unusual. In fact, they were emotionally and intellectually privileged—but not entirely.

My father, Charles Bernard Nutting, was English, Presbyterian, and Republican. My mother, Mary Agnes Flannagan, was Irish, Catholic, and Democrat. This unlikely couple met in a Greek class at the University of Iowa. They had very different backgrounds: My father's father, Charles Cleveland Nutting, was a professor at the University of Iowa. He was a scientist, what was then called a Naturalist. My mother's father had died when she was three. Her mother, Catherine Flannagan, raised Mary Agnes and her younger sister, never remarrying.

Charles and Mary Agnes did not marry until their late twenties. By that time, my father had an LL.D. degree from Harvard Law School and was beginning a career as a law professor. My mother, who had a master's degree in the classics and had been teaching Latin at Loyola University in Chicago, stopped working when she married. In later years I asked my mother why she had stopped working. She told me that during the Depression she did not think it right for a married person, whose spouse was employed, to take a job that would otherwise belong to the breadwinner of a family. There were not enough jobs to go around. I was reminded once again that my mother was a loving person, not longing for wealth or professional recognition.

I am the youngest of my parents' three daughters. I realize that in some ways the youngest is often spoiled. However, I think my sisters would agree with the way I describe our home life: I never heard an angry word between my mother and father. Neither ever yelled, at each other or at us. Each treated other people—all other people—with a kind of innate formality, a natural courtesy. Our home was filled with love.

Our everyday life was also quite formal. We had to dress for dinner every night: no shorts, pedal pushers (what are now called capris), or slacks allowed except on Saturday. Cocktails preceded dinner, in the living room. We girls could join the conversation if we wished, each having one small coke. However, we understood that this was not child-centered time.

My father always wore a coat and tie to dinner. The food was placed on serving plates at my father's end of the table. Every meal began with my father's saying his Presbyterian grace: "Bless, O Lord, these gifts to our use and us to thy loving service, through Christ our Lord, Amen." After saying grace, he would carve the meat, even if it was only spam, and dish up the plates. No one could take a bite until after my mother had started to eat. My sisters and I would not have dreamed of leaving the table without asking to be excused.

We had wonderful cocktail hour and dinnertime conversations. My parents modeled the fact that people can have conversations on topics about which they disagree without being disagreeable. Each would listen respectfully to the other's point of view. On voting days they would drive to the polls together, cancel out each other's vote, come home, and have their usual pleasant evening.

However, although we prayed together before every meal, I have no memory of my parents discussing their religious differences in the presence of the children. I remember having conversations with each of them individually about religion, but not conversations that involved the whole family. Perhaps one reason for this is that in order for my father to marry my mother he had to promise that the children of the marriage would be raised Catholic. He didn't want to do anything that would break that promise.

When my parents married, in 1933, Roman Catholics called a marriage between a Catholic and a non-Catholic (*non-Catholic* is how Catholics referred to all other Christians) a "mixed marriage." While not forbidden, such marriages were frowned upon by the Catholic Church. The ceremony itself had to be private: It took place in the rectory, not the church building.

My father was faithful to his promise to raise the children Catholic. While he himself remained Presbyterian, he was completely supportive of my mother as she raised my sisters and me in the Catholic Church. When I became an adult, I asked my father if it had been difficult for him to make and to keep this promise. He told me that it had been extremely difficult. He said that he did not think there was anything wrong with being Catholic. If he had thought that, he would not have made the promise in the first place. However, he knew that I would be taught that there was something wrong with being Presbyterian. This fact caused him great pain, especially because he was the seventh generation of faithful Protestants, all of whom had been either ministers or teachers. He said that when he made that promise, he felt that he was turning his back on his ancestors.

My father was correct in saying that I would be taught that there was something wrong with being Presbyterian. Before the Second Vatican Council (1962–1965), Catholic children were taught that only Catholics could get to heaven. In hindsight I realize that the fact that I was taught this and believed it is the backdrop for much of what I will describe as unfolding later.

From first grade, when I started to memorize the *Baltimore Catechism* (used by Catholics for children's religious education throughout the United States), I repeated to my father the questions and answers I learned. Here are some examples from *Baltimore Catechism Number 1* that my father, without comment, heard from me.

Question Number 65: "What is the Church?"

"The Church is the congregation of all baptized persons united in the same true faith, the same sacrifice, and the same sacraments, under the Holy Father, the Pope." (With this answer, my father, of course, realized that Catholics did not consider him a member of the Church because he did not recognize the authority of the Pope.)

Question Number 72: "Which is the one true Church established by Christ?"

"The one true Church established by Christ is the Catholic Church. There are hundreds of different churches in the world today, but only the Catholic Church is the one true Church established by Christ."

Question Number 91: "How does a Catholic sin against faith?"

"A Catholic sins against faith by not believing what God has revealed, and by taking part in non-Catholic worship. . . . Catholics know that there is only one true religion, and that God wants us to worship Him according to that one true religion. To take part in non-Catholic (Protestant, Jewish, etc.) worship is like saying we do not believe that there is only one true religion."

In fidelity to what the Roman Catholic Church taught at that time, my mother, sisters, and I never worshipped with my father in his church. Every Sunday we would drive to an early mass, and my father would drive to his church when we returned. If we were on a trip, my father would worship with us, but when we returned home, he returned to his own church.

As a child, I was taught and believed that because my father freely chose not to be Catholic, he could not be saved. *Baltimore Catechism Number Two* asks and answers the following questions:

Question 166: "Are all obliged to belong to the Catholic Church in order to be saved?"

"All are obliged to belong to the Catholic Church in order to be saved."

Question 167: "What do we mean when we say, 'Outside the Church there is no salvation'?"

"When we say, 'Outside the Church there is no salvation,' we mean that those who through their own grave fault do not know that the Catholic Church is the true Church or, knowing it, refuse to join it, cannot be saved."

I prayed diligently for my father's "conversion," as we called it then, even sneaking into my parents' bedroom and sprinkling holy water on his pillow. Heaven would not be heaven for me if my father was not there, too.

I was at St. Mary's College in South Bend, Indiana (1959–1963) during some of the Second Vatican Council

(1962–1965). I remember clearly that one of our teachers tried to keep us abreast of what was happening at the Council. At one point, our teacher had an ecumenist tell the class what was happening ecumenically. The ecumenist told the class that our posture in ecumenical dialogue (dialogue among Christians) could not be: "We are right and you are wrong. When you see things our way we can once more have visible unity." I remember raising my hand and asking, "How can our posture be anything else since we are right and they are wrong?"

Since the Second Vatican Council, no Catholic child would have been taught what I had been taught. As paragraph 818 of the present *Catechism of the Catholic Church,* quoting Vatican II's *Decree on Ecumenism* (*Unitatis Redintegratio*) teaches, "One cannot charge with the sin of the separation those who at present are born into these communities (that resulted from such separation) and in them are brought up in the faith of Christ, and the Catholic Church accepts them with respect and affection as brothers . . . . All who have been justified by faith in Baptism are incorporated into Christ; they therefore have a right to be called Christians, and with good reason are accepted as brothers in the Lord by the children of the Catholic Church."

Can such "brothers and sisters" be saved? Now, the answer is yes. As paragraph 819 of the *Catechism of the Catholic Church* says: "'Furthermore, many elements of sanctification and of truth' are found outside the visible confines of the Catholic Church: 'the written Word of God; the life of grace; faith, hope, and charity, with the other interior gifts of the Holy Spirit, as well as visible elements.' Christ's Spirit uses these Churches and ecclesial communities as means of salvation . . . ."

Because of the Second Vatican Council, long before my father died, I had come to understand that he and I already belonged to the same Church. Because of our mutual, ongoing personal and communal faults, that unity was not yet visible in the way we acted. However, that unity was a gift that God had already given us, and it was our job to be open to whatever conversions were necessary in order to make that unity visible.

I do not know whether or not I would have outgrown the prejudice that I had been taught as a child toward other Christians, toward other members of the body of Christ, on my own. I hope I would have, but I just don't know. As things worked out, the very Roman Catholic Church that I had loved and trusted as a child gave me permission to understand that what I had previously been taught was in error. In other words, the Roman Catholic Church acknowledged that the ongoing process of "conversion" that I prayed my father, a very loving, intelligent, and faithful person, would experience was a process that I myself, and my beloved Roman Catholic Church, needed to undergo. In order for the Church (now understood to be all of the baptized, not just Catholics), the whole body of Christ, to have visible unity, *all* must undergo a conversion of heart.

The Catechism of the Catholic Church, when speaking of the call toward unity that we believe is the will of Christ, affirms this truth in paragraph 821:

> Certain things are required in order to respond adequately to this call [i.e. the call to Christian unity]:
> —a permanent renewal of the Church in greater fidelity to her vocation; such renewal is the driving-force of the movement toward unity;
> —conversion of heart as the faithful "try to live holier lives according to the Gospel"; for it is the unfaithfulness of the members to Christ's gift which causes divisions.

Given this background, the reader can understand that, having experienced conversion in one area of my life, I was open to consider the possibility of conversion in other areas of my life as well. The Spirit blows where the Spirit wills, and all of us, individually and as communities, are involved in an ongoing process of understanding how we should live so as to be faithful disciples of Jesus Christ, faithful witnesses of Christ's good news to the world. Ever since, I have lived with the question: In what other areas of my life have I been taught prejudice, either by my Church or by my culture? In what other areas of my life am I called to conversion?

MY CALL TO STUDY, TEACH, AND WRITE ABOUT SCRIPTURE

I did not know until I began to work full-time for the Catholic Church that my having been raised in an ecumenical family gave me a unique and valuable background. Sad to say, many Roman Catholics of my generation (I was born in 1941) were warned not to read the Bible. This posture was evidently a reaction to the reformation, to vernacular translations, and to the fear of private interpretation. In fact, an *Admonition* appeared in Catholic Bibles:

> To prevent and remedy this abuse [i.e. mistaking the true sense of Scripture], and to guard against error, it was judged necessary to forbid the reading of the Scriptures in the vulgar languages, without the advice and permission of the Pastors and spiritual Guides whom God has appointed to govern his Church . . . .
>
> Nor is this due submission to the Catholic Church . . . to be understood of the ignorant and unlearned only, but also of men accomplished in all kinds of learning: the ignorant fall into errors for want of knowledge, and the learned through pride and self-sufficiency.

In obedience to this warning, many Catholics never read the Bible. They did hear out of context passages from the Bible proclaimed at mass. However, as wonderful as it is, the Lectionary (the book of readings proclaimed at mass) is not the Bible. A person whose only familiarity with biblical passages is from the Lectionary does not know the biblical context of the passage, knowledge that is essential in order to determine the inspired author's meaning.

As a young Catholic, I was completely unaware of this warning and did read the Bible, just as my father did. By the time I became an adult, the Catholic Church was teaching us that all Christians should be "nourished and ruled by Scripture" (*Dei Verbum* #21). However, many Catholics were at a distinct disadvantage in this regard because they could not be "nourished and ruled" by something they had never read.

I learned to be a biblical contextualist from the academy, not from the Church. As an English major working toward a Master's Degree in the late 1960s, I took a course in the "Bible as Literature" at the University of Massachusetts. There I learned that one could not expect to understand what an inspired biblical author is intending to teach if one does not take into consideration the literary form in which the author is writing. Later I learned that the Catholic Church agreed with this insight, and, since 1943 with the publication of *Divino Afflante Spiritu*, had officially taught the importance of understanding context when interpreting any part of the Bible.

As had been true of me, however, most Catholics were completely unaware that this was the Catholic Church's teaching. In fact, in the early 1970s, when I taught high school seniors at Lexington Catholic High School to consider context in order to understand meaning, the principal was inundated with complaints. The students' parents had never been taught what the students were now learning, and many of their parish priests had not been taught to be contextualists either. Because of the course at U. Mass., I became acutely aware of a pervasive need in the Roman Catholic Church: adult education, especially in the area of Scripture.

Having perceived this need, and knowing that I wanted to respond to it, I received some crucial advice. At the time I did not think there was anything unusual about receiving this advice. In hindsight, I think it was one more example of God's Providence.

The year before our family moved to Lexington, Kentucky, we had lived for one year in Belmont, Massachusetts, while my husband, Don, did a postdoc in Community Mental Health Delivery Systems at Harvard. Our children were 1, 3, 5, and 7. We lived in an upstairs apartment, had wonderful friends, but very little money. Since my studies were interrupted for the year, one of my teachers suggested that I spend the year writing so that I would have an intellectual pursuit that didn't cost any money. He said he would find someone to read what I wrote and give me feedback. The person he found was named Naomi Burton Stone. As I soon discovered, she was the great spiritual writer, Thomas Merton's, literary agent. All that year, out of the goodness of her heart, Naomi read what I sent her and offered me suggestions about how to improve my writing.

After my husband completed his program and accepted a job in Lexington, I was able to return to school. By then Naomi knew me and my interests very well. She advised me to get a Ph.D. in English Literature. She said that biblical scholars across denominations agree that the Bible is a library of books, not a book with chapters. However, biblical scholars and theologians often do not have the background in literature to speak with clarity about the different literary forms that are found in the Bible. If they want to say that a particular book or story is not history, they might say it is a *parable*, or a *myth*, or a *legend*, or an *allegory*, or a *fable* without knowing the differences among these literary forms. In doing so, they are muddying the waters. What the field needed was people who could speak with clarity on these issues.

Following her advice, I pursued a Ph.D. in English literature with the expressed purpose of applying my knowledge of literature to biblical texts. In the process of earning this degree I had, for the first time, an experience that was so extraordinary that I believed, right when it was happening, that God was powerful and present in the events that were unfolding.

The Ph.D. program at the University of Kentucky, where I was then studying, required students to choose three areas in which to be tested for their comprehensive exams. I chose Medieval Literature, Renaissance Literature, and Nineteenth-Century Literature. Each exam was to be three hours long on separate days. Two were to be written exams, and one oral.

In preparation for the exams, I went to the chair of the department and requested a reading list, explaining that I had been studying for eighteen years in four different geographic locations, and I thought it only fair that I be given some guidance about what might be on the test. I will never forget his answer. He said, "There is no reading list. If it's written in English it can be on your test." I came home completely discouraged and scared to death. However, soon after, I once more read the parable of the talents (Matt 25:14–30). In this parable Jesus is teaching the apostles that they must not, out of fear, simply bury their talents. They must have the courage to act. So, I decided that it would be better to take the comprehensive exams and fail than to choose failure by not trying.

I had nine months to prepare. My husband and four children all helped me by taking over many of the household responsibilities so that I could study eight hours a day. The first test was to be on the Monday after Easter. On Good Friday I remember thinking that I would just skip the Good Friday services. Then I thought, "If I die before Monday, my knowledge of Spenser's *Faerie Queene* will be irrelevant." So, I went to Church with my family. When the priest got up to give a homily I thought, "Sermons are an important literary form in Medieval Literature, and I don't know much about them." When we left Church I mentioned this to my husband. He suggested that I go to the library and get out a book on medieval sermons. I did just that and spent much of Friday and Saturday reading the book.

On Easter night, after the children were in bed, I was reviewing Chaucer notes that I had taken at St. Mary's College eighteen years earlier. On the bottom of one page there were notes on the form of a Medieval Sermon, applying the various parts of a sermon that had been explained in the book to Chaucer's *Pardoner's Tale*. The next morning I went to the University to take the test on Medieval Literature. I was to respond to three essay questions, spending an hour on each. The third essay was: Write on the allegorical and medieval sermonizing techniques in the *Friar's* and *Pardoner's Tales*. I couldn't believe my eyes. I was filled with gratitude. For the first time I felt confident that I was going to pass the test.

When I got home I told my family what had happened. I had both the notes and the test to back up this remarkable story. I also asked my husband, who is a psychologist, what he thought I should do to prepare for the next test on Wednesday on Renaissance Literature. My husband advised me not to review lots of plays but to read one book, any book, just to keep me calm and occupied. I read a book a friend had suggested I read entitled *Spenser's Faerie Queene: Continued Allegory or Dark Conceit.* After reading the book, I had six pages of notes on this topic. The next day I went in to take another three hour test. The first question was a ninety minute essay—half the test. The first topic was: "Allegory in *The Faerie Queene.*"

It is hard to describe how I felt at that moment. I was over-whelmed with a feeling of gratitude. Locked in the exam room by myself, I knelt down and thanked God for providing me with what I needed to pass the test. I felt my own efforts were not going to be enough, so God had intervened through events and lifted me over the hurdle. I would be forever grateful. I would also be for-ever mindful that whatever opportunities were mine because I had a Ph.D. were also gifts. It is certainly true that without a Ph.D. I would not have had the many teaching and writing opportunities that have come my way.

ACTS OF POWER OR MIRACLES?

Earlier I described my experience when taking my comprehensive exams as *miraculous.* By using that word I am not claiming that something supernatural occurred. I am simply claiming that I ex-perienced the event, at the time it was occurring, as one in which God's power and presence were overwhelmingly present. Wheth-er God used means that I would call *natural* or means that I would call *supernatural* is irrelevant. What is relevant is that I experi-enced God's power and presence in the event.

It was in the Bible as Literature class that I first learned this distinction between what we might call *miraculous* and what we might call *supernatural*. The Greek word for such an event is *dynameis*, the root of our word *dynamite*. The word places the emphasis on the power experienced, not on whether the event is natural or supernatural, a scientific distinction.

When teaching this concept, the professor surmised that perhaps the Exodus had been made possible by a log-jam upstream. Immediately after he said this, a young woman got up abruptly and left the class. I thought that she might be sick and might need help. So, at the break I sought her out. I found her in the lady's room, weeping. I asked her if I could help her, and she said, "That man is an atheist." I asked, "What man?" She said, "Our professor. He denies God's role in the Exodus."

I knew the professor in his usual setting, as a minister, and assured her that this was not the case. I said, "He is not an atheist. He is a Christian minister. He was not denying God's ultimate role, he was surmising about the proximate cause that God used to help the Israelites. The Israelites definitely experienced the events as events in which God was powerful and present."

It is God's power, experienced in events, that constitutes the biblical sense of God's *acts of power*. Whether, as people who live in a scientific age, we know the proximate cause or we do not is irrelevant. God can be just as powerful and present in events that we would call *natural* as God is powerful and present in events that we would call *supernatural.*

After I passed my comps I wanted to tell my friend who had given me the book about allegory in *The Faerie Queene* just what had happened. I wanted him to know that he had been an instrument of God's providence in my life. When I told him the story his response was, "Margie, you are one lucky person." I tried to explain that I did not experience it as luck. I gathered that he had not yet had a similar experience, so he was not yet willing to interpret the event as one in which God was powerful and present, nor ready to acknowledge his own role as an instrument of God's love and providence in my life.

Due to this experience, I felt very sure that God does work through events. My studies re-enforced this idea, since the first step in the formation of the Bible that we now have was people's experiences of God, powerful and present in their lives. This experience also helped me when I was serving parish evangelizers, helping them to name their own experiences of God. Perhaps it also caused me to actually look for God's presence in events as they were happening. In any event, the stage had been set for some very powerful experiences of God's presence in events.

SPIRITUAL LESSONS LEARNED / REFLECTIONS

1. I must be open to the possibility that some things I was taught and believed as a child are wrong. Both religions and cultures inadvertently teach prejudices that, as a child, I accepted but that, as an adult, I need to outgrow.

   - What prejudices have I been taught? Do I still believe them?
   - What effect does holding on to a prejudice have on others? On me? On our community?

   "When I was a child, I spoke like a child, I thought like a child, I reasoned like a child; when I became an adult, I put an end to childish ways" (1 Cor 13:11; NRSV).

2. God is powerful and present in events, events that I consider extraordinary and events that I consider ordinary. I am never alone.

   - When have I experienced God's power and presence in my life?
   - Are there events that I considered ordinary when they occurred but that I realized in hindsight were God's providence in my life? What are they?

   "I will never forsake you or abandon you" (Heb 13:5b).

3. I must not, out of fear, refuse to do that which I feel called
   to do. It is better to try and risk failure than to choose failure
   by being afraid to try.

   - Has fear prevented me from doing what I feel called
     to do? In what ways?
   - How might I replace that fear with trust?

   "Even though I walk in the dark valley, / I fear no evil; for
   you are at my side" (Ps 23:4).

4. My work opportunities and successes are not so much ac-
   complishments as they are gifts. They should never become
   a source of pride but always be a source of gratitude.

   - What circumstances resulted in my having the work I
     do have? Do I see God's hand in these circumstances?
     In what ways?
   - What gifts have I received personally that make me
     capable of doing my work? Do I see these gifts as gifts
     from God given to me for the purpose of serving oth-
     ers? Do I thank God for these gifts?

   "As each one has received a gift, use it to serve one another as good stewards of God's varied grace" (1 Peter 4:10).

2

APPROACHING THE VEIL TOGETHER

My father had his first stroke at 70. At the time he was a law professor at Hastings Law School in San Francisco. Due to his health, at the end of the academic year, my father retired. He and my mother moved to Lexington, Kentucky where my husband, Don, and I lived with our four children. I was extremely grateful that my parents moved to Lexington. I wanted our children to have the benefit of knowing their grandparents on a daily basis.

However, I think the move was very difficult for my father because it involved his giving up his life's work as well as the respect and recognition from others that are the natural consequence of a long life of service to others. (In addition to being a law professor, my father had been Dean of two law schools as well as Vice Chancellor and Acting Chancellor of the University of Pittsburgh.) Giving up his professional identity was a kind of death all by itself.

My parents moved into a condominium in walking distance from our home. For a few years after the move, both of my parents were relatively healthy and were able to take care of themselves. However, my father had another stroke, which resulted in my mother's having to hire people to help her take care of him. This was another small death for my father because the kind of care he needed violated his sense of dignity. By the time both of my parents had died, some of their caretakers had been employed by them for over ten years.

It is easy enough to see God's hand in events when events are experienced as blessings, as they were when I passed my comprehensives. It is another thing entirely to believe that God is present, loving, and powerful when we witness a loved one suffering. Why would God allow my father and mother to go through such a long, painful ordeal during their last years on earth? This question constantly presented itself to my mind. But then I would ask: Why would God allow his own son to be crucified? Why would God allow poor Mary to witness her son being crucified as a criminal when he was so young? To watch a child suffer and die prematurely had to be much more painful than to watch an elderly parent die. Why is death part of the order of things?

Perhaps because of the home in which I was raised, I could not refrain from asking the questions. However, I had already accepted the fact that I am part of a pilgrim Church, that my own knowledge and my Church's knowledge and ability to understand are limited, and that I, as well as my Church, are called to new understandings. Also, because of the home in which I was raised, as well as my own marriage and children, I knew with absolute certainty that love exists. I already treasured that passage of Scripture that allowed me, in my experience of having been loved all my life, to begin to probe the mystery of God as love: "God is love, and whoever remains in love remains in God, and God in him" (1 John 4:16). So, as my parents' last, painful years approached, I was prepared to enter the mystery.

A final stroke resulted in my father's being unable to walk, talk, swallow, or communicate in any way. He appeared to be in a coma. The events that have had such a profound effect on my life occurred in these last weeks of his life. By that time, my mother was herself not well and so was not able to be with my father when he was in the hospital, nor able to make decisions on his behalf. Therefore, those responsibilities fell to me.

After this totally disabling stroke, the doctors wanted me to sign a paper, right then and there, giving them permission to pro-

vide my father with a surgically implanted feeding tube. From
their point of view, this was routine for a person who was unable to
swallow. However, I agonized over the decision. I wanted to do
what my father would have done if he had been able to make the
decision for himself, but I didn't know what his decision would
have been. I wanted to sign the paper if it would prolong my
father's life, but I did not want simply to prolong his dying. I knew
that my own Roman Catholic tradition taught that one need not
choose to use extraordinary medical options, but inserting a feeding tube, even though it was a surgical procedure, was not considered extraordinary. I also did not know whether or not my father's
having a feeding tube would affect my parents' ability to continue
to live together. None of our caretakers were nurses, nor was I.
Would we be able to take care of my father if he returned home?
Not knowing what to do, I signed the papers.

Immediately after signing the papers I got on the elevator at
the hospital. Since I was upset and close to tears I did not look
around. I just entered and faced front. After the doors closed, a
woman's voice behind me said, "I don't think you recognized me."
I turned and looked at the woman. As far as I knew, I had never
seen her before. I said, "I'm sorry, but I do not recognize you."
She said, "Well, that's no wonder. When you give a talk on Scripture everyone knows who you are, but you don't know all of us. I
heard you speak on a contextualist understanding of Scripture at
Christ the King. I love your work."

I thanked the woman, and, just to say something, I said, "What
is your work?" She said, "I work for Option Home Care. Have you
ever heard of us?" I said I had not. She replied, "Well, this is just a
for-instance: But say someone has had a stroke, and that person
needs a feeding tube, and the family wants to take care of that
person at home. We go to people's homes and teach them how to
do that."

I couldn't believe what I was hearing. I looked at her and said,
"That is exactly our situation. I just signed the permission for my
father to receive the feeding tube. We do want to take care of him
at home, but my mother is not well herself, and our caretakers are

not nurses." Seeing my distress, she replied, "Now don't you worry about this. If your father returns home, we will come to your parents' home and teach everyone how to take care of him with the feeding tube."

My father did return home, and Option Home Care did send someone to my parents' home to teach everyone how to take care of him with the feeding tube. However, four weeks later, my father developed a high fever, due to pneumonia, and had to return to the hospital.

After my father had been in the hospital for a few days, I noticed that his lips and tongue were getting a little crusty. I thought he wasn't getting enough moisture in his mouth. I mentioned this to his nurse. She must have been having a bad day because her response was about how demanding families are and how understaffed hospitals are. Once more, I was close to tears, left the room, and got on the elevator. The doors on the elevator shut, and the whole elevator shook. I thought it had moved and that I might be stuck between floors. However, when the doors opened I was still on the same floor. Not wanting to take any more chances with the elevator, I exited and started walking down the stairs. I was only about half a flight down when a woman's voice behind me said, "I don't think you recognized me." I turned to face the woman and acknowledged that I did not recognize her. She said, "Well, I think it was at least fifteen years ago. But I took a Scripture course from you. I love Scripture." I, of course, remembered what had happened only four weeks earlier. So, I asked, "What do you do?" She replied, "I supervise the nursing care of geriatric stroke patients."

I was dumbfounded. Could this be happening twice? It seemed it was. I quickly told the woman that I was having a problem with the nursing care of a geriatric stroke patient right that minute. She listened carefully and then said, "I don't want you to worry about this. I am going to go to your father's room right now and take care of it." That is exactly what she did.

My thoughts about this experience at the time had to do with God's provident care. Here I was, not knowing what was best, making important decisions for my parents, and just praying that I would make the right decisions. Then these two women arrive on the scene. Each identifies her connection with me to be Scripture. Each listens to my father's needs and takes care of them. The women were like angels, messengers from God, assuring me that God was present, that God was loving and caring for my father.

My father did not recover or return home. About four weeks later, he died in the hospital. I tried to visit him four times a day: on my way to work, at lunch, on my way home, and after dinner. I wanted with all my heart to be with him when he took his last breath. I prayed for that privilege constantly.

The final four weeks were very tense. However, they did have their lighter moments. At the time all of this was happening, I was the Secretary of Educational Ministries for the Diocese of Lexington. We were a close-knit group of colleagues, and, when we were not on the road serving parishes, we had lunch together. Each day when I returned from my noon visit to the hospital, the lunch group would want to know how things had gone. Since I had given them a daily report, they all knew about what we referred to as "the elevator stories."

One day my daily report was about a question I had been asked by one of the nurses. As I explained to my colleagues, I had been sitting next to my father's bed, holding his hand. He was unable to respond in any way. At the time, I was 51 and my father was 86. A young nurse came into the room and attempted to make friendly conversation. She asked me, "Are you his wife or his sister?" I was horrified: His wife or his sister! I must look awful! When I got to this part of the story, one of my colleagues stopped me and said, "Let me guess what happened next. You entered the elevator, close to tears. The doors closed. A woman's voice behind you said, "I don't think you recognized me." You turned, but did not recognize her. You said, "What do you do?" She said, "I am a beautician." Despite my grief, we all had a wonderful laugh then, and I have been smiling ever since when I remember the third "elevator story."

One late morning I received a call at work that my father's death appeared to be imminent. I immediately called my husband, Don, and we each left work and rushed to the hospital. I was very grateful that when I arrived at my father's room, he was still alive. I don't know why, but I had my heart set on being with him when he took his last breath. My husband understood this and wanted to be with me as, for the first time, I experienced first hand the death of someone I loved deeply.

Six hours later, Don and I were still sitting by the bedside, watching every breath that my father laboriously took. About that time a priest who was a colleague of mine from the diocese and a friend of both my husband and mine came to keep vigil with us. This priest had played a vital role in my father's story earlier (to be explained), and he knew all that had already happened.

Six hours later, the three of us were still keeping vigil. The priest said to me, "Margie, you need to get some sleep." I explained that I did not want to sleep. I had been fervently praying that I would have the privilege of being with my father when he took his last breath. I did not want to be absent simply because I had fallen asleep. The priest said, "I will sit next to your father with my hand on his wrist, feeling his pulse. If anything changes I will immediately wake you."

So, still holding my father's hand, I put my head on the railing of his bed and immediately fell into a deep sleep. Sometime later I heard a voice call me. The voice simply said, "Margaret," in an urgent tone. I was immediately wide awake. I looked at Don and said, "Did you call me?" He said, "No, I did not call you." I looked at our priest friend and asked, "Did you call me?" He was still sitting there with his hand on my father's wrist. He said, "No, I did not call you." I said, "Well, someone called me." Then, I looked at my father. He took one breath and then stopped breathing. He was no longer living on earth.

SPIRITUAL LESSONS LEARNED / REFLECTIONS

1. It is fine to ask questions, even if I do not immediately find answers. Questions are not doubts. They are steps to a deeper understanding of the truth.

   - Do I feel free to ask hard questions based on my experience?
   - What questions do I want to ask? Where might I seek answers?

   "My God, my God, why have you forsaken me?" (Ps 22:1; Mark 15:34).

2. God is love. As long as I am acting in love I am on the right path, even if I do not understand why things are happening as they are.

   - Do I truly believe that God is love, even when I am suffering?
   - Do I believe that God, in God's love, will give me the gifts I need—the strength and the wisdom—to choose wisely for others when I am praying to love faithfully and to do God's will?

   "God is love, and whoever remains in love remains in God, and God in him. . . . There is no fear in love, but perfect love drives out fear . . . . We love because he first loved us" (1 John 4:16, 18,19).

3. Suffering is a mystery. When love demands that we enter the mystery of suffering, we must do just that.

   - When suffering is unavoidable, am I willing to endure it in order to remain faithful in love?
   - When I embrace unavoidable suffering, do I trust that God is still with me and that some kind of good is being accomplished through the painful experience?

"My soul is sorrowful, even to death. . . . He advanced a little and fell to the ground and prayed that if it were possible the hour might pass by him; he said, 'Abba, Father, all things are possible to you. Take this cup away from me, but not what I will but what you will'" (Mark 14:34, 35–36).

4. When in doubt, choose life.

- Do I truly believe that life is a gift from God and that God has a purpose in each person's life?
- Do I trust that if I choose life, God will act for my loved one's good?

"I call heaven and earth today to witness against you: I have set before you life and death . . .Choose life" (Deut 30:19)

5. Christ is present through his body, the Church. When I am feeling alone it is often because I have failed to recognize Christ in others.

- Do I believe Christ's promise that he will be with us always?
- Do I treat people with openness so that they can be other Christs for me?

"And behold, I am with you always, until the end of the age" (Matt 28:20).

6. Friends, work, laughter, and normalcy are a great comfort in times of grief.

- When I am grieving, do I let other people in?
- Am I willing to share my burdens as well as my joys with those who love me?

"Blessed are they who mourn, for they will be comforted" (Matt 5:4).

7. God does answer prayer.

- Do I believe that God's answer to prayer is either, "yes," or, "I have a better idea"?
- Do I believe that God loves both me and the person for whom I am praying and will accomplish good in every situation, even if God's way of doing that is beyond my comprehension?

"Ask, and it will be given you; seek and you will find; knock, and the door will be opened to you" (Matt 7:7).

3

THE FUNERAL: LONG-TERM PLANNING ON GOD'S PART

One day, many years after my parents' move to Lexington, but only a few years before my father's final stroke, my father spoke to me about his funeral. He told me of two ministers from his Presbyterian Church whom he admired, either of whom I could contact to make arrangements when that time came, one a man and one a woman. I already knew both of these ministers because of my involvement with the Kentucky Council of Churches. However, I knew the woman better than the man.

I first met this wonderful woman, whom I will call Beth, at a Kentucky Council of Churches meeting. We were using our yearly Assembly meetings to study the BEM (*Baptist, Eucharist and Ministry*) document, a 1982 document prepared by the World Council of Churches' Commission on Faith and Order. In 1985 we were devoting our yearly meeting to the topic of Eucharist. As part of our shared experience, we celebrated the Lima Liturgy, an ecumenical Eucharistic service. I was attending the Assembly as a representative of the Diocese of Covington.

We Catholics were instructed to attend the service and to take part in any way we could—for instance, as lectors—but not to receive Eucharist. The reason was that the Catholic Church teaches that Eucharist is a sign of full unity, a unity that we had not yet achieved. As representatives of the diocese, our behavior was to give witness to that teaching. I was thrilled to be involved in this worship service and in the discussions that followed. To worship with Christians who were not Catholic was a new and liberating experience for me. At that time, I did not find it painful to refrain from receiving Eucharist. However, I noticed as I remained in my chair that Beth found our actions terribly painful. When she returned from Eucharist she looked at me, and there were tears streaming down her face.

Several years later, Beth contacted me and asked if I would teach a Bible class at the Presbyterian Church, my father's church, where she was now the minister. I knew where it was, but I had never set foot in the building. I readily agreed. Beth attended the course with many in her congregation, and, over the weeks, we became closer and closer.

After we had formed a bond of trust, Beth asked if she could visit me at my office at the Catholic Center. She had something she needed to talk over. When Beth arrived, she again started to cry. She explained to me that she has a deep hunger for Eucharist and for church unity. Her Presbyterian Church celebrated Eucharist only four times a year. She knew that the Catholic Church celebrated Eucharist every day. She believed that Christ was truly present in Eucharist. Her question was whether or not she could receive Eucharist at a Catholic mass during the week and still remain a faithful Presbyterian minister to the flock she was presently serving.

Beth and I continued to meet once a week for several weeks. In the meantime, I inquired of our diocesan Ecumenical Officer (the same priest who would later be with us at my father's deathbed) if such a thing were possible. He assured me that if the person was sincere, if the person believed in Christ's presence in Eucharist, and if the person had no way of satisfying her hunger for Eucharist in her own denomination, then, with permission, an exception could be made, and she would be invited to the Eucharistic table before full unity is achieved between our churches.

It wasn't long before Beth was ready to act: I introduced her to our Ecumenical Officer; he sought the proper permission from the Pope's delegate in Washington, D.C.; and she was quietly welcomed to the Eucharistic table at daily mass. At the same time, she continued to serve as pastor of her Presbyterian Church. This went on for some years. Only after she had fulfilled all her responsibilities in regard to her ordination and had retired from active ministry did she formally and publically come into full union with the Catholic Church. At the time my father died, Beth was a retired Presbyterian minister and an active Roman Catholic.

During the last few months of my father's life, I began to think more about his funeral. I remembered what he had told me about his two favorite ministers, but the man had moved out of town, and the woman was now Catholic. While I was pondering what to do, without having come to any decision, I attended an ecumenical study day sponsored by the Diocese of Lexington. The program was intended to be an ongoing education day for our priests, but, because he knew of my deep interest in ecumenism, our Bishop invited me to come, too. When I arrived I stood at the door to the auditorium and looked over the group, sitting at round tables for eight. The Bishop saw me, came over, and said, "I know just what you are doing. You're looking over the group to see who you already know so that you can have a good time with old friends. However, that's not why I invited you. Look over the group and point to someone you don't already know." I pointed to a complete stranger. The Bishop said, "Good. Come over and I'll introduce you."

After the introductions, I realized that the person to whom I had pointed had a parallel position in the Presbyterian Church to the position that the Bishop had in the Roman Catholic Church. He wasn't called *Bishop* but *Executive Presbyter*. This man welcomed me to his table and engaged me in conversation during breaks and during lunch. As the day progressed I found myself telling him about my father, his approaching death, and his desire to have one of the two ministers he admired preside. I ended by saying, "But I don't think that will work out because one has left town and the other is now a Roman Catholic. I realize I couldn't ask her, as a Catholic, to preside at my father's funeral in his Presbyterian Church." The Executive Presbyter replied, "I wouldn't have a problem with it." I wasn't sure I had heard him correctly. I said, "What did you just say?" He assured me, "I wouldn't have a problem with Beth presiding at your father's funeral in a Presbyterian Church even though she is now in full communion with the Roman Catholic Church. Why don't you ask her and see how she feels about it." I did ask her, she readily accepted, and that is exactly what happened.

The funeral was the first time in our lives that my father's whole family had been together in his Church. I knew that my mother was finding the whole situation very painful, not just because my father had died, but because he had not become Roman Catholic. I thought God had arranged things to comfort her. So, just before the funeral began, I said to my mother, "You see that minister? She's Catholic." My mother didn't think she had heard me correctly. She asked, "What did you say?" I replied, "I said that the minister is a Catholic. I think God is trying to tell us something. I think that minister symbolizes the fact that you and Dad belonged to the same Church all these years, the one body of Christ. It's just that Catholics and Presbyterians have not yet learned to live so that our unity is visible." My mother looked at me with what I thought was a hopeful expression. She replied, "Margaret, you do have some very unusual ideas."

The minister, Beth, understood the situation she was in and responded in a beautiful way. She knew the pain of Christians being divided. That is why she had been crying at the Lima Liturgy. She was comfortable in a Presbyterian Church full of Roman Catholics. Since my parents had not lived in Lexington until after their professional lives were over, most of the people in the Church were my family's friends and my colleagues from the diocese. Beth realized that she was talking to the leaders of many of the diocesan offices as well as some parish priests.

Beth first talked about the long, loving, marriage my parents had had. She said, "This couple truly loved each other. They had children together. They had professional lives that served their communities. They lived lovingly with each other for sixty years. They believed in the same God. They believed in Jesus Christ. They had the same value system. They took care of each other in every way. But there was one thing they could never do together. They could never receive Eucharist together. That's right. They could never receive Eucharist together. Whose fault is that?" Her voice dropped, and with deep sadness she asked once more, "Whose fault is that?"

Our diocesan leaders were already being urged to take the scandal of Christian Church divisions seriously, and we were being educated on the topic so that we could act in ways that promoted visible unity. However, none of our past in-services on ecumenism had had the emotional impact that Beth's sermon had. Divisions are a scandal. They do cause real pain. They do prevent Christians from being the witnesses of Christ to the world that we are each called to be.

Even more important to me, personally, is that I think both Beth's presence and her words gave my mother great comfort in the days to come. My parents had loved each other deeply for sixty years. They did worship the same God and live in fidelity to the teachings of Jesus Christ. They were not only one body in marriage, but, through baptism, they were both part of the body of Christ. That Presbyterian/Catholic clergywoman *was* a living symbol of God's revelation to my mother. My father *was* safe in God's hands, and it would not be long before my mother, too, would pass through death to new life. Heaven *was* going to be heaven for her because my father *was* going to be there.

A MASS FOR MY FATHER

Because I served all the parishes in the Diocese of Lexington in my role as Secretary of Educational Ministries, many of the parish leaders reached out to me to comfort me when my father died. The Newman Center at the University of Kentucky had a mass for my father. They sent me a written notice, and I arranged my schedule so that I could be at the mass.

When I arrived on the date that the invitation named, the priest said, "Oh, Margie. I'm so pleased to see you. I'm glad you could be with us today. We said the mass for your father yesterday, but we are happy to have you here today." I was chagrined, but thanked him for yesterday's mass and said I was happy to be with them, too.

I went into Church and prepared to celebrate mass. As I sat there, I remembered how grateful I was that I had been in town, with my father, and awake when he took his last breath. I vividly remembered the voice that woke me with its urgent "Margaret!" I remembered that I asked Don if he had called me, and he had said no. I asked the priest if he had called me, and he had said no. Soon after, the lector got up and read the first reading. It was 1 Samuel 3:1–10.

> During the time young Samuel was minister to the Lord under Eli, a revelation of the Lord was uncommon and vision infrequent. One day Eli was asleep in his usual place. His eyes had lately grown so weak that he could not see. The lamp of God was not yet extinguished, and Samuel was sleeping in the temple of the Lord where the ark of God was. The Lord called to Samuel, who answered, "Here I am." Samuel ran to Eli and said, "Here I am. You called me." "I did not call you," Eli said. "Go back to sleep." So he went back to sleep. Again the Lord called Samuel who rose and went to Eli. "Here I am," he said. "You called me." But Eli answered, "I did not call you, my son. Go back to sleep." At that time Samuel was not familiar with the Lord, because the Lord had not revealed anything to him as yet. The Lord called Samuel again, for the third time. Getting up and going to Eli, he said, "Here I am. You called me." Then Eli understood that the Lord was calling the youth. So Eli said to Samuel, "Go to sleep, and if you are called, reply, 'Speak, Lord, for your servant is listening.'" When Samuel went to sleep in his place, the Lord came and revealed his presence

calling out as before, "Samuel, Samuel!" Samuel answered, "Speak, for your servant is listening."

Ever since, I have believed that when God calls me by name, God calls me "Margaret." I have also believed that my posture toward God and God's self-revelation in Scripture must be one of listening: Like Samuel, I am to say, "Speak, for your servant is listening." Now, as one who listens carefully to God's word in Scripture, I would like to share with you some of what I have heard.

SPIRITUAL LESSONS LEARNED / REFLECTIONS

1. Receiving Eucharist both expresses unity and effects unity in the body of Christ.

   • Is refraining from inviting other Christians to Eucharist at a Catholic mass faithful to Jesus's will for his body, the Church?
   • Is declining to receive Eucharist in other Christian Churches faithful to Jesus's will for his body, the Church?

   "First of all, I hear that when you meet as a church, there are divisions among you . . . . A person should examine himself, and so eat the bread and drink the cup. For anyone who eats and drinks without discerning the body, eats and drinks judgment on himself" (1 Cor 11:18, 28–29).

2. All who are baptized into the body of Christ are already one Church. We just refuse to act so as to make this unity visible.

   • Do I hold on to prejudices against other Christians? What is my reason for doing this?

- What could I do to make the unity of Christ's body, the Church, more visible?

"I . . . urge you to live in a manner worthy of the call you have received, . . . striving to preserve the unity of the spirit through the bond of peace: one body and one Spirit, as you were also called to the one hope of your call; one Lord, one faith, one baptism; one God and Father of all, who is over all and through all and in all" (Eph 4:1, 3–6).

3. God has called me by name. I am constantly to listen and to be attentive to God's voice.

   - How does God speak? Through Scripture? Through Church tradition? Through other people? Through nature?
   - How can I hear God's voice more clearly? Through prayer? Through study? Through faith sharing?

"Speak, Lord, for your servant is listening" (1 Sam 3:9).

4. God's provident love is operating in our lives constantly, through what appear to be routine events.

   - Am I willing to trust that God is lovingly present in my life even when I do not feel that presence?
   - Am I willing to trust that God is lovingly present in my life even when the events of my life cause me to suffer?

"God is our refuge and our strength, / an ever-present help in distress. / Therefore we fear not, though the earth be shaken, / and mountains plunge into the depths of the sea" (Ps 46:1–2).

4

DISCERNING CHRIST IN THE WHOLE BODY OF CHRIST

The spiritual lessons learned from the events surrounding my father's death dawned on me slowly over the following years. True, I had undergone a great deal of internal conversion before my father's death. I had realized that what I had initially been taught about other Christians was simply wrong. I had come to understand that Catholics and other Christians are all part of the one Church, the one body of Christ. To finally realize that what I had been taught, had believed, and had acted upon was simply a prejudice opened my mind to the possibility that my worldview might include other prejudices that I had not yet recognized.

In addition, I had experienced the two women saying, "I don't think you recognized me," and had interpreted their presence as an expression of God's own presence and God's providential love and care. Also, shortly after the funeral, after hearing the reading from 1 Samuel while attending mass at the Newman Center, I had realized that my posture in God's presence, God's self-revelation in Scripture, and God's presence in the events of my life, must be one of listening.

So, as I went about living my normal life: taking care of my family, serving the parishes, and teaching Scripture, I found, to my joy and amazement, that I was seeing meanings in Scripture that I had previously not seen.

PAUL'S TEACHING ON EUCHARIST

I had heard many times Paul's account of Jesus's instituting Eucharist on the night before he died. In a Catholic setting, the following passage is proclaimed on Holy Thursday Mass in all three years of the liturgical cycle in the *Lectionary* (the book that contains the readings from Scripture that are proclaimed at mass. In the Catholic Church the *Lectionary* is based on a three-year cycle.)

> For I received from the Lord what I also handed on to you, that the Lord Jesus, on the night he was handed over, took bread, and after he had given thanks, broke it and said, "This is my body that is for you. Do this in remembrance of me." In the same way also the cup, after supper, saying, "This cup is the new covenant in my blood. Do this, as often as you drink it, in remembrance of me." For as often as you eat this bread and drink the cup, you proclaim the death of the Lord until he comes. (1 Cor 11:23–26)

While this selection from 1 Corinthians is perfectly appropriate for a Holy Thursday celebration, the few verses read do omit the context in which the passage appears in 1 Corinthians. To understand the context we must read what comes before and after this passage. Before describing Jesus at the last supper Paul says:

> First of all, I hear that when you meet as a church there are divisions among you, and to a degree I believe it . . . . When you meet in one place, then, it is not to eat the Lord's supper, for in eating, each one goes ahead with his own supper, and one goes hungry while another gets drunk. Do you not have houses in which you can eat and drink? Or do you show contempt for the church of God and make those who have nothing

feel ashamed? What can I say to you? Shall I praise you? In this
matter I do not praise you. (1 Cor 11:18–22)

When we hear these verses we realize that Paul is admonishing
the Corinthians because when they come together to celebrate
Eucharist in each other's homes as part of a shared meal, they are
ignoring the poor in their midst.

After the Holy Thursday passage Paul goes on to say:

> Therefore, whoever eats the bread or drinks the cup of the
> Lord unworthily will have to answer for the body and blood of
> the Lord. A person should examine himself, and so eat the
> bread and drink the cup. For anyone who eats and drinks with-
> out discerning the body, eats and drinks judgment on himself.
> (1 Cor 11:27–29)

As a Catholic who believes in Christ's real presence in Eucharist, I had always thought that the words, "without discerning the
body" referred to that real presence. I thought the passage was
teaching that a person who does not believe in the real presence
should not receive Eucharist.

Certainly, Paul believes that Christ is present in Eucharist. He
obviously had taught the Corinthians of Christ's real presence
when he was with them for eighteen months during his second
missionary journey (see Acts 18:1–28) because Paul assumes that
the Corinthians know this. Earlier in 1 Corinthians Paul has asked,
"The cup of blessing that we bless, is it not a sharing in the blood
of Christ? The bread that we break, is it not a sharing in the body
of Christ?" (1 Cor 10:16).

However, that is not what Paul is teaching when he warns the
Corinthians that "whoever eats the bread or drinks the cup of the
Lord unworthily will have to answer for the body and blood of the
Lord," and that "anyone who eats and drinks without discerning
the body, eats and drinks judgment on himself" (1 Cor 11:27–29).
In this passage the body to which Paul is referring is the body of
Christ that is the Church. The parts of the body of Christ that the
Corinthians are not discerning are the poor in their midst. By

mistreating the poor, the Corinthians are responsible for the body and blood of Christ.

Where did Paul get such an idea? How did Paul learn that Jesus identifies so thoroughly with his followers that the way a person treats one of Jesus's disciples is the way one is treating Jesus himself? We need look no further than Paul's conversion story to see where Paul learned this profound truth. We read three accounts of Paul's call story in the Acts of the Apostles (Acts 9:1–19; 22:1–16; 26:9–18). While the accounts differ in details, they all tell the same core story: Paul is surrounded by a bright light and hears a voice ask, "Saul, Saul, why do you persecute me?" Paul asks, "Who are you, Lord?" The voice responds, "I am Jesus, whom you are persecuting" (Acts 9:3–5).

Jesus did not ask Paul, "Why do you persecute my followers?" Rather, Jesus asked, "Why do you persecute me?" Ever after, Paul understood that Jesus identifies totally with his disciples. After all, Paul had persecuted Jesus's followers and had participated in Stephen's death (see Acts 7:58–8:3). Having done that, and having heard Jesus's question to him, Paul knew exactly what it was to fail to discern the body and so to be responsible for the body and blood of Christ. Paul didn't want the Corinthians to make the same mistake.

Paul, therefore, became a witness to two core truths of the Gospel: First, he knew that Jesus had risen from the dead and was alive and present. In addition, he understood that those who were baptized into Christ's body and who received Christ's body at Eucharist became what they received: the body of Christ. Paul did not want the Corinthians to fail to see Christ in the poor, to fail to discern the body. It is as though Paul were helping the Corinthians hear the words I heard from the two women at the hospital when my father was dying. However, now the words were on the lips of the risen Christ: "I don't think you recognized me."

"LORD, WHEN DID WE SEE YOU HUNGRY?"

Matthew's Gospel also teaches that the way one treats the hungry, the thirsty, the stranger, the naked, the ill, and the prisoner is the way one is treating Christ. Matthew does this through picturing Jesus telling the parable of the judgment of the nations (Matt 25:31–46). This parable is part of the longer eschatological (about the end times) discourse that Jesus gives to the disciples (24:1–25:46). The setting is judgment time. The king who judges rewards those who cared for him when he was hungry, thirsty, and naked by inviting them into the kingdom. They ask, "Lord, when was it that we saw you hungry and gave you food, or thirsty and gave you something to drink?" (Matt 25:37). The king replies, "Truly I tell you, just as you did it to one of the least of these who are members of my family, you did it to me" (Matt 25:40, NRSV).

This passage is particularly interesting because it pictures those who care for the ones in need and are rewarded as not recognizing that they are serving their king by serving the poor. Still, their good works result in their being invited into the kingdom. It seems that Jesus is teaching the disciples that as long as they care for the marginalized, they will be invited into the kingdom even if they have failed to recognize that in doing so they are serving Christ. When Christ welcomes such disciples into the kingdom, I imagine Christ saying, "I don't think you recognized me."

LACK OF RECOGNITION IN THE POSTRESURRECTION APPEARANCE STORIES

Lack of recognition is a recurring theme in the postresurrection appearance stories. Although the stories differ greatly in plot, both Luke and John include stories in which those who know and love Jesus fail to recognize the risen Christ in their midst. For years, as I taught these stories, I had the nagging feeling that I didn't really understand them. I would ask myself: "How could Jesus's disciples on the road to Emmaus fail to recognize him for a whole day?"

(Luke 24:13–35). Or, "How could Mary Magdalene, who loved Jesus with all her heart, possibly have mistaken him for a gardener?" (John 20:15). Or, "Out of all the disciples, why does only the beloved disciple initially recognize Jesus when he sees him on the shore?" (John 21:1–14). However, when I read these stories in the light of my new experiences, I began to think I was asking the wrong questions. The question that I should be asking is, "What were Luke and John teaching their audiences, and us, by telling these stories in the way they did?"

TWO DISCIPLES ON THE ROAD TO EMMAUS

Only Luke tells us the story of the two disciples on the road to Emmaus (Luke 24:13–35). Mark, one of Luke's sources, does mention that Jesus "appeared in another form to two of them walking along on their way to the country. They returned and told the others; but they did not believe them either" (Mark 16:12–13). As I read Luke's story now, I think that Luke has dramatized the event mentioned in Mark in order to teach his audience, Gentiles in about 85 A.D., the ways in which the risen Christ is in their lives, perhaps unrecognized.

As the account begins, the two disciples are walking along, dejected and disappointed because their hopes that Jesus would be their messiah and return home rule to the Israelites had been dashed. Instead of prevailing over the Romans, their hoped-for messiah had been crucified by the Romans. Luke tells us that "while they were conversing and debating, Jesus himself drew near and walked with them, but their eyes were prevented from recognizing him" (Luke 24:115–116). Here Luke is teaching the same truth that Matthew teaches when he pictures Jesus saying, "For where two or three are gathered together in my name, there am I in the midst of them" (Matt 18:20). The two disciples are gathered in Christ's name, and Christ is with them. The same thing is true for us. However, like the two disciples on the road to Emmaus, our eyes are often prevented from recognizing him.

Jesus then joins the two disciples and becomes their fellow traveler. The two welcome this stranger, not realizing that in doing so they are welcoming Jesus himself. They pour out their disappointment to Jesus. They speak of their dashed hopes and of their hesitancy to believe the good news that the women have given them. We know that the two disciples did not believe the women's report that "they had indeed seen a vision of angels who announced that [Jesus] was alive" (Luke 24:23) because they are still dejected. They have no idea that the very Jesus for whom they are looking is present in their fellow traveler. Once more, Matthew teaches the same thing when the king in Jesus's parable says, "I was a stranger and you welcomed me . . . . " He tells the nations that, "Just as you did it to one of the least of these who are members of my family, you did it to me" (Matt 25:35, 40; NRSV), even though they were unaware that in doing so they were serving their king. The same thing is true in our lives. When we welcome our fellow travelers, the strangers in our midst, we are welcoming the risen Christ.

Luke then pictures Jesus saying to the two disciples what Luke is saying to his audience and to us, "Oh, how foolish you are! How slow of heart to believe all that the prophets spoke" (Luke 24:25). Jesus then opens the Scripture for them, allowing them to see a meaning in the texts that they had failed to see before: Jesus "interpreted to them what referred to him in all the scriptures" (Luke 24:27).

Luke does not tell us which passages Jesus interpreted as referring to himself. However, the Church also opens the Scripture during the Lectionary cycle and shows us texts that the Church hears as referring to Jesus, texts such as Isaiah's messianic prophesies (Is 7:10–14, 9:1–7, 11:1–9) that we proclaim during Advent and 2 Isaiah's suffering servant songs (Is 42:1–7, 49:1–7, 50:4–9, 52:13–53:12) that we proclaim during Holy Week. (We will have occasion to probe some of Isaiah's prophesies in future chapters because, as we will see, some of them directly address the mystery of suffering.) In using Scripture in this way the Church is hearing the words of the prophets as a living word.

In fact, the Catholic Church teaches that the risen Christ is present in the word proclaimed. Indeed, Christ himself is proclaiming the word: "When the Scriptures are read in the church, God himself is speaking to his people and Christ, present in his own word, is proclaiming the Gospel" (*General Instruction on the Roman Missal*, n. 29). Through the Church, the body of Christ, the risen Christ interprets Scripture for us just as Christ did for the disciples on the road to Emmaus. However, our eyes, too, are often prevented from seeing the risen Christ in our midst.

The two disciples did not recognize Christ's presence until Jesus "took bread, said the blessing, broke it, and gave it to them. With that their eyes were opened and they recognized him, but he vanished from their sight" (Luke 24:30–31). Those of us who have been raised Catholic have certainly been taught to recognize Christ's presence in Eucharist. However, is it not also true of us that once we recognize Christ, Christ vanishes from our sight? Once we walk out of the church door, do we continue to recognize the presence of the risen Christ when two of us are gathered together, in the stranger on the road, and in the Scripture? Or, do we fail to recognize Christ? If so, Christ is saying to each one of us: "I don't think you recognized me."

LACK OF RECOGNITION IN JOHN'S POSTRESURRECTION STORIES

The lack of recognition theme continues in John's Gospel, first with the story of Jesus's appearance to Mary Magdalene (John 20:11–18). Again, in order to understand what John is teaching, instead of asking, "Why couldn't Mary Magdalene recognize Jesus, whom she loved and for whom she was looking?" we should ask, "What is John teaching his audience by telling the story this way?" John is writing for end-of-the-first-century Jewish Christians who are also longing to see the risen Christ. They had expected the Son of Man to return on the clouds of heaven long before their time, and they are asking, "Where is the risen Christ?" John is answering that question throughout his Gospel. He is also answering that question in his "lack of recognition" postresurrection appearance stories.

Mary Magdalene is weeping by the tomb. Both the angels at the tomb (John 20:13) and the unknown man, whom she takes to be a gardener (John 20:15), ask her, "Why are you weeping?" Mary Magdalene is weeping because she thinks that Jesus is dead, that Jesus is no longer present, that she can no longer be in relationship with him. Only when Jesus calls her by name (John 20:16) does she recognize that Jesus is still alive and with her.

In the context of John's Gospel, this scene is an allusion to a previous scene: Jesus's teaching on himself as the good shepherd. Jesus says, "I am the good shepherd. And I know mine and mine know me, just as the Father knows me and I know the Father: and I will lay down my life for the sheep" (John 10:14–15). Mary Magdalene belongs to Jesus's flock. She recognizes Jesus when he calls her by name: "The sheep hear his voice, as he calls his own sheep by name . . ." (John 10:3).

I, too, have been called by name: "Margaret!" This fact became crystal clear to me during mass at the Newman Center shortly after my father's death when I heard the reading from 1 Samuel. However, it was just as true before I had that experience. I have been called by name my entire life. So has each one of us. The question is: Do we recognize the voice of the person who is calling?

Once Mary Magdalene recognizes her friend and teacher, she clings to him. Jesus does not want her to cling to their old way of being in relationship but to leave him free to return to his Father. Jesus says: "Stop holding on to me, for I have not yet ascended to the Father" (John 20:17). This, too, is true of all of us who have lost loved ones. We are not to cling to them. We are to leave them free to move on to the next stage of life, knowing that they are in the hands of God who loves them like a parent: Jesus says: "I am going to my Father and your Father, to my God and your God" (John 20:17).

Mary Magdalene is then given a mission: She is to be a witness of her own experience of the presence of the risen Lord. In fidelity to Jesus's instructions, "Mary of Magdala went and announced to the disciples, 'I have seen the Lord,'" (John 20:18). Mary's words, "I have seen the Lord" will become a refrain in John's postresurrection appearance stories. That is exactly what John wants his end-of-the-century audience to be able to say. The risen Lord is not missing in action. Rather, the risen Lord is present. John wants his readers to recognize that Jesus is already in their midst.

DOUBTING THOMAS

In John's Gospel, Jesus's postresurrection appearances are not teaching us that Jesus, soon after his resurrection, was only occasionally present with his disciples, that he came and went. Rather, the stories are teaching that Jesus is always present with his disciples, but that his presence is not always manifest to them.

This is clearly the case in the story of doubting Thomas. When Jesus appears to the disciples on Easter eve, Thomas is not with them. The other disciples tell Thomas, "We have seen the Lord." Thomas declares: "Unless I see the mark of the nails in his hands and put my finger into the nailmarks and put my hand into his side, I will not believe" (John 20:25). A week later, Jesus again appears to his disciples, and this time Thomas is present. Jesus says to Thomas, "Put your finger here and see my hands, and bring your hand and put it into my side, and do not be unbelieving, but believe" (John 20:27). Notice, Jesus was not pictured as present when Thomas had doubted. However, Jesus is fully aware of everything that was said in his perceived absence. Obviously, Jesus was not absent at all, but was always present. It is just that the disciples sometimes perceived that presence and sometimes did not.

This is true of our lives, too. Occasionally we have an experience that is so overwhelming that we can think of no explanation for what has happened other than a vague, "Someone was watching out for me." Those of us who think in religious categories of thought might say that our guardian angels were on the job, or that someone in the communion of saints was taking care of us, or that the risen Christ was with us. These are wonderful experiences, and they confirm our faith. However, the presence of the Lord that appears to be manifest in those rare events is just as true on a day-to-day basis. The risen Lord is always with us, but sometimes we fail to recognize him.

JESUS'S APPEARANCE AT THE SEA OF TIBERIAS

John continues his lack of recognition stories with Jesus's third appearance to the disciples, this time on the shore of the Sea of Tiberias. Here, a character unique to John's Gospel appears, a character who is never named but is called *the beloved disciple* or *the disciple whom Jesus loved*. As is often the case, the beloved disciple appears with Peter and realizes the truth before Peter does. This was true after Mary Magdalene told the beloved disciple and Peter that Jesus's tomb was empty. The beloved disciple and Peter both ran to the tomb; the beloved disciple got there first but waited respectfully for Peter to catch up before he entered the tomb. Both entered the tomb, but the beloved disciple was the first to believe (see John 20:1–10).

The beloved disciple is also the first to recognize that the man on the shore who directed the disciples to cast their net on the right side of the boat is the Lord: "So the disciple whom Jesus loved said to Peter, 'It is the Lord'" (John 21:7). Simon Peter believes the beloved disciple and jumps into the sea in his eagerness to be with the Lord. As Jesus offers the disciples some bread, they all recognize who it is that is caring for them and feeding them: "Jesus said to them, 'Come, have breakfast.' And none of the disciples dared to ask him, 'Who are you?' because they realized it was the Lord" (John 21:12).

Scripture scholars surmise that the reason John pictures the beloved disciple and Peter together, and the beloved disciple always arriving at the truth first, is that John's community emphasized love over authority. The beloved disciple symbolized the priority of love. Peter symbolized duly delegated authority. Both arrive at the same conclusions, but love gets there first. Jesus is feeding and caring for his disciples whether they recognize him or not. However, one is more likely to recognize the presence of the risen Lord when one is acting in love.

THE PRIORITY OF LOVE IN THE BODY OF CHRIST

Paul, nearly a half century before John's Gospel was written, also taught the priority of love. We have already discussed Paul's admonishing the Corinthians that when they ignored the poor in their midst, thereby not recognizing Christ's body, and then received Eucharist, they had eaten the bread and drunk the cup unworthily and so would "have to answer for the body and blood of the Lord" (1 Cor 11:27). Paul then goes on to describe the unity and variety of gifts that have been given to the Church community by the Holy Spirit. Paul says, "As a body is one though it has many parts, and all the parts of the body, though many, are one body, so also Christ. For in one Spirit we were all baptized into one body, whether Jews or Greeks, slaves or free persons, and we were all given to drink of one Spirit" (1 Cor 12:12–13). After reminding the Corinthians of the need the whole body has for each individual part, Paul says, "Now you are Christ's body, and individually parts of it" (1 Cor 12:27).

While all gifts given to the body of Christ are necessary, Paul insists that love is the most important gift that the Holy Spirit has given the Church. Paul even goes so far as to say: "And if I have the gift of prophecy and comprehend all mysteries and all knowledge; if I have all faith so as to move mountains, but do not have love, I am nothing. If I give away everything I own, and if I hand my body over so that I may boast but do not have love, I gain nothing" (1 Cor 13:2–3).

What Paul teaches the Corinthians is just as true for us today. As members of Christ's body, we have all received gifts that we are to use in service to others. In doing so, we are being Christ for others and seeing Christ in others. However, we will succeed in doing this only to the extent that we act in love. Those who act in love are more likely to be the first to say, "It is the Lord," rather than to hear, "I don't think you recognized me."

SPIRITUAL LESSONS LEARNED / REFLECTIONS

1. The way I treat other people is the way I am treating the risen Christ.

    - What specifically do I do to help the poor?
    - How do I serve other marginalized people?

    "Truly I tell you, just as you did it for one of the least of these who are members of my family, you did it to me" (Matt 25:40; NRSV).

2. When interpreting Scripture I must remember to ask, "What is the inspired author teaching by telling the story this way?"

    - Do I change the subject by asking questions about history or science rather than by asking questions about our relationship with God?
    - What does Scripture teach me about my relationship with God? About my relationship with God's other beloved children?

    "A lamp to my feet is your word / a light to my path. / I resolve and swear, / to keep your ordinances. . . . / Deal with your servant according to your kindness / and teach me your statutes" (Ps 119:105–106, 124).

3. Christ is present, even when I am grieving and feeling Christ's absence, not his presence.

- Do I recognize Christ in my fellow travelers on life's journey?
- Do I recognize Christ in Scripture? In Eucharist?

"With that their eyes were opened, and they recognized him . . . . Then they said to each other, 'Were not our hearts burning [within us] while he spoke to us on the way, and opened the scriptures to us?'" (Luke 24:31, 32).

4. Jesus calls each person by name.

- In what ways have I been called? By Baptism? By a heart's longing? Through friendships?
- To what have I been called? To know Jesus? To serve others? Based on my gifts, how specifically have I been called to serve?

"The Lord called me from birth, / from my mother's womb he gave me my name" (Is 49:1b).

5. I must not cling to those who are dying, but leave them free to go to God.

- What does it mean not to cling to those who are dying?
- Does my behavior leave my loved ones free to move on?

"Stop holding on to me, for I have not yet ascended to the Father" (John 20:17).

6. I am to be a witness to the risen Lord.

- When and how have I "seen the Lord"?
- How do I share this good news with others?

"Thus it is written that the Messiah would suffer and rise from the dead on the third day and that repentance, for the forgiveness of sins, would be preached in his name to all nations, beginning from Jerusalem. You are witnesses of these things" (Luke 24:47–48).

7. In the whole body of Christ, love is most important.

- Do I love my fellow Christians of all denominations?
- What behaviors of mine give witness to this love?
- What behaviors of mine fail to give witness to this love?

"So faith, hope, and love remain, these three; but the greatest of these is love" (1 Cor 13:13).

5

BEING THE BODY OF CHRIST

After my father's death, the words, "I don't think you recognized me" were a constant reminder to me that I was to see Christ in others. However, it is just as true that we are to be Christ for others. Over the years, I think my parents' caregivers began to see Christ in them. On several occasions, the circumstances of my father's death put me in a situation in which, in hindsight, I realized that I had had the privilege of being Christ for others, and they had been Christ for me.

MY PARENTS AS OTHER CHRISTS

Both of my parents were very kind, very intelligent, very gentle, and very loving. When my mother first hired caretakers to help her take care of my father, she was fairly healthy herself. The people she hired were not skilled nurses. They were simply warm-hearted people who could do things for my father that my mother was not strong enough to do. My mother had a tendency to treat the caretakers as guests in her home. She never treated them simply as functionaries who were physically stronger than she was. The caretakers found her innate courtesy and gentleness extremely endearing. They also found the way my parents treated each other inspiring.

My mother lived five years after my father died, and the caretakers took care of her, just as they had taken care of my father. One young woman, whom I will call Cindy, had never met anyone like my mother. On the other hand, my mother had never met anyone like Cindy. Cindy was from a background very different from mine. She had very little education. At a very young age she had married unwisely, and her husband was in prison.

The more time my mother spent with Cindy, the more she grew to admire her. Over and over she would say to me, "That Cindy is smart as a whip!" My mother had taught Latin in college (at Loyola in Chicago before her marriage and at The George Washington University after her three daughters had left home). She remembered all she had taught and thought Cindy might like to learn a little Latin. I think Cindy agreed to this just to give my mother something to do, but she was an apt student. Over and over my mother, with great admiration, would tell Cindy: "You are smart as a whip! You could do anything you want to do."

After watching this relationship of mutual admiration for years, I was well aware that Cindy's life circumstances had deprived her of the kind of education that she would have received and benefited from had she been my parents' child. I now know that this truth became evident to Cindy, too. In addition, Cindy realized that it was not too late to do something about that.

My first hint of the profound effect my parents had had on Cindy came shortly after my mother's death. My sisters and I invited the caregivers to come to my parents' home and select things to keep that had special meaning for them. Most selected china, glasses, or jewelry. Not Cindy. She wanted, of all things, my father's old briefcase. So, that is what we gave her.

I had no contact with Cindy for some time after that last meeting. However, two years after my mother's death, Cindy called me up. She told me that my parents' lives had had a profound effect on her, that after my mother had died she had returned to school, and she invited me to her graduation from junior college. I went with great gratitude and pride: gratitude that Cindy had been motivated to build on her God-given gifts, and pride that my parents, especially my mother, had instilled in her the confidence to do it.

That Cindy really was as smart as a whip!

COMFORTING WORDS OF BELIEF

After one of my father's strokes, but not the one that led to his death, my father had to spend several nights in the hospital. A caretaker, whom I will call Cathy, stayed with my father in the hospital. I came by after dinner, and we spent several hours alone together while my father was sleeping. By then we were quite confident that my father would be coming home again. Cathy used this occasion to ask me a number of questions about my work for the Church, my beliefs, and particularly my beliefs about suffering and death.

I explained to Cathy that I believe that the most important part of God's self-revelation through Jesus Christ, revealed to us in Scripture, is that God is love. Love is the core of Jesus's message. Therefore, our goal in life should be to become loving people.

In addition, Jesus revealed that life does not end with life on earth. Jesus's postresurrection appearances persuaded the first generation Church not only of Jesus's identity as the Son of God, but also of the reality of life after death. Just as Jesus passed through death to life, so will we. So, I believe that when our loved one's leave earth we can still be in relationship with them. We just relate in a different way.

Based on Jesus's example, we don't choose suffering or death, but, at the same time, when we have no choice, we must accept it. Jesus didn't choose the cross. He chose to be faithful to his vocation and his love for God. The unavoidable ramification of those loving choices was the cross. God can redeem every situation, and good can be the final result of our accepting suffering. We can learn a great deal from the more difficult experiences in our lives.

I believe that, while God does not will sin or suffering, depending on the way we respond to them, even these experiences can have a positive outcome in our lives.

Cathy had not come from a religious family, and she was hungry to hear more. In both Cathy's and my minds, the context for this conversation was my parents' suffering and my father's death. However, the next morning we heard that Cathy would not be able to come to work that afternoon. Why? Because her father had died suddenly the previous night.

I saw Cathy the next afternoon at the funeral home. We just hugged each other while she wept. There was no need for words. We both believed that the Holy Spirit had been taking care of Cathy by inspiring all her questions during our late night conversation, just hours before her own father died.

YOU HAVE BEEN FORGIVEN

During my father's last hospitalization, for some of the time he had a roommate. One difficulty with sharing a hospital room is that you cannot help overhearing what is going on with the other patient. My father was unable to communicate, so he was not a companion for the man who lay ill on the other side of the curtain. On several occasions while sitting with my father and holding his hand, I overheard the man in the next bed cry out in an agonized voice, "Oh God, forgive me." This didn't happen every time I was there, but over several days I heard this agonized plea over and over: "Oh God, forgive me."

As I sat in the hospital room I couldn't stop thinking about this situation. I began to have a new appreciation for the sacrament of reconciliation that Catholics celebrate. It is a wonderful thing to hear that one is forgiven and to believe it. A minister visited the man in the next bed, but the cries for forgiveness were not uttered in his presence, only after he left. I began to long to have the man hear that he was forgiven. I, of course, had no idea what he had done to cause such agony. However, I believe that Jesus taught us that all repentant sinners are forgiven.

This truth is particularly emphasized in Luke's Gospel. In Luke, Jesus's words on the cross are words of forgiveness. Even while he was being crucified Jesus says, "Father, forgive them, they know not what they do" (Luke 23:34). In addition, Jesus forgives a man who was also being crucified right after the man has admitted that he deserves the punishment he is receiving. Jesus tells the man, "Today you will be with me in Paradise" (Luke 23:43). When Jesus commissions the disciples, he tells them that, "repentance for the forgiveness of sin would be preached in [Jesus's] name to all the nations, beginning from Jerusalem" (Luke 24:47). I was sure that the risen Christ wanted my father's hospital roommate, who had repented, to hear that he was forgiven.

Later that evening I asked my psychologist husband if he thought I would do the man any harm if I told him he was forgiven. Don didn't think I would be doing harm. The next day at work I asked our priest friend if he thought I would be doing any harm. He did not. After praying about this, I decided that I would do nothing if I heard nothing from the man. However, if he cried out, I would walk around the curtain that divided the beds and tell him that he has been forgiven.

The next night the agonized cry once more filled the room, "Oh God, forgive me." I stood up, walked around the curtain and said: "I have a message for you." The man looked frightened. I repeated, "I have a message for you. Can you hear me?" He nodded. I said, "You have been forgiven." His eyes grew wide. I repeated, "Can you hear me? You have been forgiven." He nodded, and I went back around the curtain to my father's bedside.

The next day there were no agonized cries. The day after that the bed was empty. I asked the nurse what had happened to the patient in the next bed. She said, "Yesterday he seemed much better and was able to eat on his own. Today he went home."

I have no way of knowing if the man's health improved dramatically because he believed he was forgiven. However, I suspect that was the case. Guilt is a terrible burden. Repentance is the result of a person's having accepted constantly offered grace. The fact that God always loves the sinner and forgives the repentant sinner is also core to the Gospel.

HOLY HUMOR

In my mother's last year she did not have Alzheimer's, but there were occasions when she was disoriented. During those times she still had her usual personality: kind, formal, smart; but she was definitely disoriented.

One morning when I dropped by she told me that she wanted me to think of something special we could do for Cindy. She told me that on the night before there had been a civil war going on outside with lots of gun shots, that Cindy could have fled for her life, but she did not. Cindy had stayed right with her through it all.

On another occasion, soon after my sisters, both of whom live out of town, had visited, my mother told me: "I have seen Catherine and Elizabeth recently, but I have not seen Margaret in quite some time." I responded, "I am Margaret." She said, "I mean my daughter Margaret." I said, "I am your daughter Margaret." She looked at me reproachfully and said, "My daughter Margaret is a great deal younger than you are." After seeing the expression on my face, my mother wanted to comfort me. She said, "If you are my daughter Margaret I must have two daughters by that name. I wonder why we would have named two daughters Margaret?" I said, "I am your daughter Margaret, and I am the only Margaret." Again, she looked at me reproachfully and said, "I don't think you have any right to claim sole ownership of that name."

Occasions like this are sad. It is hard to have your mother not realize you are her daughter. At the same time, I couldn't help but see some humor in the situation. Perhaps that was a defense mechanism: I would rather laugh than cry. However, when I told other people about these incidents, I felt guilty, as though I were speaking unkindly about my mother. I mentioned this feeling to an elderly Jesuit priest who had the reputation of being a wise counselor. He asked if I had seen how my mother acted when her mother was in her nineties. I have clear recollections of my mother and her sister telling stories about Grandma and laughing wholeheartedly. I never doubted for one moment that they loved their mother. The priest said, "Your mother shared your sense of humor. I think she would understand perfectly why you choose to laugh rather than cry. Think of it as one of the last gifts she can give you." I treasured that advice, and I agreed with it. To be able to see humor even in painful situations is a gift—a gift we should embrace always, especially in difficult times.

THE COMMUNION OF SAINTS

Having been raised in the Roman Catholic Church, I grew up believing in the communion of saints. The idea that a person who is no longer living on earth is still alive, is part of the *Church Triumphant*, and is sharing in communion with the pilgrim church on earth was simply a given. In the liturgy we celebrated numerous saints, especially Mary. We often heard stories about the lives of the saints. The idea of asking a saint to help me with something was as natural to me as asking someone on earth to help me.

This belief that those who precede us in death are still aware of us and are part of our lives undoubtedly affected the way I interpreted something else I remember about events when my grandmother was near death. My mother told me that near the end of her mother's life, my Grandma kept insisting that her long-deceased mother (my great grandmother) had visited with her, comforted her, encouraged her, and complimented her. This was a routine claim. The visits always had a positive effect, and my grandmother would tell my mother about them with no more surprise than if my great grandmother had simply lived down the street.

In my mother's last months, this same phenomena occurred. My mother would tell me that she had visited with her mother and that her mother was very proud of her. She had a sense of her mother's presence as a routine matter. For instance, one evening I was watching a television program with my mother. She said, "Margaret, your grandmother is in the next room. Would you please go and tell her about the program we are watching, and invite her to join us? Tell her that I think she would very much enjoy both the plot and the costuming." I had no sense of my grandmother's presence, but I did exactly as my mother asked. I think as my grandmother and mother approached their deaths, the veil between this life and the next became thinner and thinner for them. I believe each of their mothers was lovingly caring for them during their last days on earth.

A PRAYER ANSWERED ONCE MORE

As was the case when my father died, I wanted to be with my mother when she took her last breath. That I would have this privilege was not a given. At the same time that my mother was slowly failing, my work required me to travel quite a bit: to California, to Chicago, and to Ohio. After the experience I had had with my father, I was at peace just leaving the course of events in God's hands. I prayed for this privilege, and believed that God's answer would be yes if being there was best for my mother.

On a Saturday evening when I was in town, the caretaker called me and told me that she thought my mother had a fever, but she couldn't take her temperature because the thermometer had been broken. I went to the drugstore, bought a thermometer, and took it over to the caretaker. My mother was asleep when I arrived. I visited with the caretaker for a while, and then went back home.

The next morning, Sunday, my husband, Don, and I agreed to take turns going to mass in case my mother needed anything. Don told me if there was an emergency he would come and get me. At mass I prayed that my mother would be at peace in her heart and soul, knowing that she was loved. I prayed, "Please pick up my mother in your arms. Hold her close to your heart. Let her know how deeply she is loved: by you, by Dad, by my sisters and their families, by me and my family, by her mother and father, by her caretakers, by everyone who has known her."

When I arrived home Don met me at the door, hugged me, and said, "The caretaker did call just a few minutes ago. Your mother is very near death." We were at my mother's home in five minutes. When I arrived, a hospice worker who had been called said, "Your mother still has a very weak pulse." I called a priest who came immediately and gave my mother the sacrament of anointing. In addition to calling us, the caretaker had called the other caretakers, who loved my mother so dearly. They all came immediately. We were all there, loving her, as my mother's pulse weakened and then stopped.

As we stood around my mother's deathbed, one of the caretakers, tears streaming down her face, said to me, "Why do you think your mother clung to life on earth so long? Do you think it was for us?" No words could have expressed more clearly to me that my mother had been Christ's presence in the lives of those who took care of her. Both through her example and through her words, she had been a blessing in the lives of those who knew and loved her.

LIFE AFTER DEATH

Perhaps it is because I teach Scripture that people tell me remarkable stories about their own lives, thus becoming witnesses of Christ's good news in my life. They know I won't dismiss what they say as nonsense. Because I have heard their stories, I know that many people believe in life after death not as a matter of faith or creed but because of their own personal experiences. Some people who do not believe in life after death discount these stories as products of the brain. However, in some cases, such an explanation simply doesn't work because the people who had the experiences and who told me their stories received objective verification of the reality of what had occurred.

For instance, one woman whom I taught in a Scripture class told me what had motivated her to go back to school. She had had a very troubled relationship with her mother. When her mother died unexpectedly, a million issues were unresolved. The daughter simply couldn't find any peace. She was filled with anger at her mother and guilt for being so angry. She became ill, sought therapy, took a leave of absence from her work and family to seek solitude: nothing helped. However, one night after she had returned home, she had what she took to be a vivid dream. In the dream, her younger son was sitting on the floor, and her mother was sitting in the rocking chair. The mother told the daughter that she was now in a good place, that all was forgiven, and that she wanted her daughter to know this so that she would not continue to suffer.

When the woman woke up, the dream was just as vivid as it had been while she was sleeping. Far from having trouble remembering it, she could think of little else. She did not immediately tell anyone about this experience. She wanted to give herself time to process it. However, later that day, the son who had been in the dream said, "We had a good visit with Nana, last night, didn't we?" The child then proceeded to tell the mother just what Nana had said.

By the time I heard this story the woman had regained her health and had started pursuing degrees in theology and psychology. She was positive that she had had the experience, but she longed to understand more about how such an experience was possible. I told her that the apostles must have felt just the same way during Jesus's postresurrection appearances. More than one of them had the experience, so they could believe that the experience was real, not a dream. The apostles, too, needed to be reconciled with Jesus because they had been estranged when Jesus died. They had deserted Jesus in his hour of greatest need.

Believing in life after death is core to the good news of the Gospel and core to our hopes for our loved ones and for ourselves. That someone is no longer living on earth does not mean that it is too late to be reconciled with that person. What a great gift it was for this once-suffering daughter to know this to be true. Also, what a great gift this daughter gave me by telling me her story. I will discuss more firsthand life after death encounters that people have shared with me in chapter 8 when I attempt to integrate the many spiritual lessons learned through these profound experiences.

IT'S A DOG'S LIFE

This last anecdote is so strange I hesitate to include it. However, I know that there are many people who have had similar experiences. There has to be an explanation, but I don't know what it is.

One night during my father's last hospitalization I returned home about 10:00 p.m. I had not yet walked that day; I am supposed to walk two miles a day as therapy for an injured back. So, I decided to walk just in our own neighborhood. Soon after I started, a dog I had never seen before came up and started to walk with me. Wherever I went, the dog went too, just as if I had him on a leash. This had never happened before, and it has never happened since.

After about forty minutes, a man on a bicycle carrying a leash rode by. He stopped on the street and called the dog to come to him. The dog would not leave me. He called again. The dog wouldn't budge. I said, "Is this your dog?" The man said, "Yes it is. I don't know why he isn't coming to me." I said, "Well, since the dog is sticking with me, how about I walk to you and then you can put on his leash." That is what we did. I walked over to the man, the dog stayed right with me, and the owner put on his leash.

Ever since this experience I have thought that dogs must have some special sense that lets them know when a person is in distress or grief. I think the dog wanted to comfort me or protect me. He wouldn't go to his owner because the job wasn't finished. I do not know how dogs fit in to God's plan for all of creation, but I now think they have a unique role to play. It appears that a person's *best friend* is very much a friend to those in need.

I think if St. Francis, who had such a deep sense of God's presence in all of creation, had had this experience, he would have addressed the dog with deep respect as *brother dog,* and thanked the dog for accompanying him. Unfortunately, that thought did not occur to me until several years later.

SPIRITUAL LESSONS LEARNED / REFLECTIONS

1. Many people have God-given gifts that have not yet been tapped. They may be unaware of their gifts or lack confidence to offer them in service to the community.

   - Do I affirm the gifts of others when I observe them?
   - Do I try to nurture the gifts of disadvantaged people personally? Through public policy?

   "Since we have gifts that differ according to the grace given to us, let us exercise them: if prophecy, in proportion to faith; if ministry, in ministering; if one is a teacher, in teaching; if one exhorts, in exhortations; if one contributes, in generosity; if one is over others, with diligence; if one does acts of mercy, with cheerfulness" (Rom 12:6–8).

2. We never know when someone else truly needs to hear the good news of the Gospel.

   - Am I willing to share my beliefs with others, especially those who ask?
   - Am I able to name in simple language the core truths of the Gospel? What are they?

   "You are witnesses of these things" (Luke 24:48).

3. God forgives repentant sinners. So must I.

   - Am I willing to acknowledge my own sins, repent, and receive forgiveness?
   - Am I willing to offer forgiveness to others, especially those who have hurt me personally?

"And forgive us our sins, for we ourselves forgive everyone in debt to us" (Luke 11:4).

4. To be able to laugh in painful times is a comfort and a gift.

- Am I willing and able to accept the gift of laughter?
- Am I willing and able to accept this gift even when it is my own behavior that has prompted it?

"A joyful heart is the health of the body, but a depressed spirit dries up the bones" (Prov 17:22).

5. Just as Christ rose from the dead, so do our loved ones. We can still be in relationship with those we love after they no longer live on earth.

- Do I truly believe in the good news of life after death?
- Do I, through prayer, stay in communion with my loved ones who have died?

"But we do not want you to be unaware, brothers, about those who have fallen asleep, so that you may not grieve like the rest, who had no hope. For if we believe that Jesus died and rose, so too will God, through Jesus, bring with him those who have fallen asleep" (1 Thes 4:13–14).

6

AN EXPLANATION FOR MY HOPE

In the last chapter, I described a situation in which one of my father's caretakers had asked me about my work for the Church and about my beliefs, especially my beliefs about death and suffering. I gave only a brief response to that question in chapter 5, since the point of the chapter was not to explain the reasons for my hope, but to give an example of people being Christ in each other's lives.

In this chapter I would like to give a more extensive answer to Cathy's questions. We are encouraged in 1 Peter to "always be ready to give an explanation to anyone who asks you for a reason for your hope, but do it with gentleness and reverence . . ." (1 Peter 3:15–16). I think the most gentle way to give an explanation for one's hope is simply to speak as a witness, not to admonish others as to what they should feel or think.

My hope is based on two things: my knowledge of Scripture and my personal experience. Each confirms the other. The hope that is mine is based primarily on Scripture, which teaches us that there is life after death and that suffering has a purpose. What I have learned from Scripture has been confirmed in my life experience.

WHY TRUST SCRIPTURE?

Before describing the hope that Scripture offers us, I think I should explain why Scripture has authority in my life. For some, the answer to this question is self-evident. They believe that Scripture is God's self-revelation and that, in a sense, because God inspired the human authors, God is the author of Scripture. They do not need to be persuaded that Scripture, when interpreted in context (see the Introduction and Appendix 1), teaches eternal truths about our relationship with God and about the ultimate meaning in life.

However, for others, this is a crucial question. They ask: Why should we care what happened four thousand to two thousand years ago? Why should we take as authoritative books that were written by superstitious, prescientific people? Why should we take as authoritative books that are copies of the originals, written by scribes who felt free to "correct" what they were copying? What could the ideas of these ancient, naive people possibly have to do with our advanced scientific culture? Those of us who value Scripture and consider it a source of invaluable wisdom need to be able to "give an account" not only of our hope, but of our reasons for trusting Scripture in the first place.

For me, the fact that Scripture was written by people who lived in a prescientific culture is irrelevant. Why? Because Scripture is not teaching science. We already mentioned this fact in our Introduction and in Appendix 1 when we named the contexts in which we must place Scripture passages in order to understand them. We do not put the authority of Scripture behind topics that the inspired authors are not addressing, such as the shape of the earth or the amount of time it took for material forms to come into being.

What topics *are* the inspired authors addressing? They are offering us insights in response to such questions as: Who is God? Who are we in relationship to God and each other? How can we live so as to please God and cooperate with the coming of God's kingdom? The Bible offers us the wisdom of two thousand years of experience in regard to these questions.

The Bible is a gift given to us by God through the Church, the community of believers. It is the end result of a five-step process, starting with events through which God revealed God's self to God's people. The events that underlie the biblical texts start with the call of Abraham, around 1850 B.C. and conclude with the spread of the Church around the then known world, in the early second century A.D.

Throughout this two-thousand-year period, people probed the meaning of the events they had experienced through stories. The stories were at first oral; later they were written down. Stories were edited in the light of subsequent events, and new writings probing the meaning of events, written in a variety of literary forms, were added to the collection. That is why we can see a growth in understanding over centuries. People grew in their understanding over time and in the light of subsequent events, just as we do.

The books in the Old Testament revolve around the Israelites' understanding of having been called into a relationship of covenant love with God, and how their experiences over centuries refined and expanded their understanding of God's love and God's purposes. The books of the New Testament revolve around the fulfillment of God's self-revelation, Jesus Christ, and what God has accomplished and is accomplishing through Christ on behalf of the whole world.

The Bible became the Bible not because the authors claimed to be inspired but because believing communities over generations found certain writings nourishing to their faith and affirming of their beliefs and experiences. They proclaimed these writings when they gathered for worship. The writings were experienced as a living word and the worshipers understood that they were part of the story. Through Scripture, God was calling and forming God's people, revealing God's love for them and God's saving actions on their behalf.

So, we don't turn to Scripture for answers to scientific questions: How old is the earth? What is the relationship of the planets to each other? How are material beings related to each other? Rather, we turn to Scripture to probe theological and spiritual mysteries: Who is God? How are we related to God? Why are we here? What is the purpose of life? What is a life well lived?

If these are the kinds of questions for which we seek answers, we could turn to no better source of wisdom than the Bible. The Bible teaches us what we need to know for right living in the kingdom of God, both on earth and in the life to come.

LIFE AFTER DEATH

The primary belief revealed in Scripture that gave me great hope while I was accompanying my parents to their deaths is that life does not end with life on earth. I am firmly convinced that there is life after "death." In this chapter I will discuss the scriptural evidence for such a belief. In chapter 8, I will give evidence from experience that reenforces this belief.

Life after Death in the Old Testament

As is true on many topics, Scripture reveals a process of coming to an understanding of life after death. From the time of Abraham (1850 B.C.) until about two hundred years before Jesus's birth, the prevailing view of the Israelites was that no life occurred once a person had died. The place of the dead was called *Sheol*. Sheol was a place of darkness; a lifeless place.

The book of Job, probably written in the sixth century B.C., reflects Israel's beliefs. Job, in the midst of his suffering, does not have hope in a life after death. Job laments,

> If I look for the nether world as my dwelling,
> if I spread my couch in the darkness,
> If I must call corruption, 'my father,'

> and the maggot 'my mother' and 'my sister,'
> Where then is my hope,
> and my prosperity, who shall see?
> Will they descend with me into the nether world?
> Shall we go down together into the dust? (Job 17:13–16)

Job's only hope seems to be that at some point his reputation will be restored on earth, and that Job will have some knowledge of this. Job says,

> But as for me, I know that my Vindicator lives,
> and that he will at last stand forth upon the dust;
> Whom I myself shall see:
> my own eyes, not another's shall behold him,
> And from my flesh I shall see God. (Job 19:25–26a)

We know that this passage does not suggest a belief in life after death because, as the story continues, it is clear that Job looks forward only to death: "Indeed I know you will turn me back in death / to the destined place of everyone alive" (Job 30:23). The book as a whole certainly does not reflect a belief in life after death. In the overall plot of the book, Job's reward for virtue is on earth, not in a life after death.

We also have clear evidence that there was no prevailing belief in life after death by the third century B.C. In the book of Ecclesiastes (also called *Qoheleth;* attributed to Solomon because of his reputation for wisdom), the author reflects on much of what he has been taught and finds these teachings lacking because they are not affirmed by experience. In the midst of explaining that "all is vanity" the author says, "For the lot of man and of beast is one lot; the one dies as well as the other. Both have the same life-breath, and man has no advantage over the beast; but all is vanity. Both go to the same place; both were made from the dust, and to the dust they both return" (Eccl 3:19–20). The only advice the author can offer, given the vanity of life, is to enjoy the simple pleasures of everyday life, to enjoy all of God's present gifts, gifts that will soon be gone.

However, in the two hundred years before Jesus's birth, some inspired authors began to hope for life after death. Their affirmation that there is life after death does not rest on what human beings have accomplished or earned, but on God's loving nature. God could not allow the fate of a person who has chosen good and the fate of a person who has chosen evil to be the same.

A belief in life after death is clearly reflected in 2 Maccabees. This book is thought to have been written about 124 B.C. The setting of the book is a little earlier, 180–161 B.C., when the Jews were suffering persecution under Antiochus IV Epiphanes. This book is part of the Catholic and Orthodox canons, but is not part of the canon of the Jewish Scripture nor of other Christian Bibles.

In 2 Maccabees, after being victorious in battle through God's intervention, the military leader of the Jewish troops, Judas Maccabeus, prays and makes a sin offering for some soldiers who had died in battle. Those soldiers were found to have been wearing "amulets sacred to the idols of Jamnia, which the law forbids the Jews to wear. So it was clear to all that this was why these men had been slain" (2 Mac 12:40). The text of 2 Maccabees goes on to say:

> The noble Judas warned the soldiers to keep themselves free from sin, for they had seen with their own eyes what had happened because of the sin of those who had fallen. He then took up a collection among all his soldiers, amounting to two thousand silver drachmas, which he sent to Jerusalem to provide for an expiatory sacrifice. In doing this he acted in a very excellent and noble way, inasmuch as he had the resurrection of the dead in view; for if he were not expecting the fallen to rise again, it would have been useless and foolish to pray for them in death. But if he did this with a view to the splendid reward that awaits those who had gone to rest in godliness, it was a holy and pious thought. (2 Mac 12:42b–45)

Obviously, there would be no reason to pray for a dead person unless one believed in a life after death.

The book of Wisdom, also called the *Wisdom of Solomon* and written in the first century B.C., clearly expresses a belief in life after death. (This book, too, is part of the Catholic and Orthodox canons, but not part of the canon of the Hebrew Scripture nor of other Christians Bibles.) This inspired author's words are familiar to many of us because they are often proclaimed at funerals:

> But the souls of the just are in the hand of God,
> and no torment shall touch them.
> They seemed, in the view of the foolish, to be dead;
> and their passing away was thought an affliction
> and their going forth from us, utter destruction.
> But they are in peace.
> For if before men, indeed, they be punished,
> yet is their hope full of immortality;
> Chastised a little, they shall be greatly blessed,
> because God tried them
> and found them worthy of himself.
> As gold in the furnace, he proved them,
> and as sacrificial offerings he took them to himself. (Wis 3:1–6)

By the time of Jesus's public ministry, the Jews disagreed on this question. The Pharisees did believe in life after death; the Sadducees did not. We see Paul take advantage of this disagreement when he is on trial before the Sanhedrin:

> Paul was aware that some were Sadducees and some Pharisees, so he called out before the Sanhedrin, "My brothers, I am a Pharisee, the son of Pharisees; [I] am on trial for hope in the resurrection of the dead." When he said this, a dispute broke out between the Pharisees and Sadducees, and the group became divided. For the Sadducees say that there is no resurrection or angels or spirits, while the Pharisees acknowledge all three. (Acts 23:6–8)

Life after Death in the New Testament

The whole New Testament—the Gospels, the Acts of the Apostles, the Letters, and the book of Revelation—affirm the same core good news of Jesus Christ: Jesus conquered death, freed human beings from slavery to sin, invited everyone into the kingdom of God, and taught us how to live so as to cooperate with the coming of God's kingdom, not thwart it. A belief in life after death is core to Christianity.

Life after Death in the Gospels

In all four Gospels, Jesus is crucified, dies, and after Jesus is dead his apostles claim that he is still alive. While no story claims that anyone witnessed the actual resurrection, all four Gospels claim that the resurrection occurred, through empty tomb stories and through postresurrection appearance stories. We have already discussed examples of postresurrection appearance stories in chapter 4. Here we will take note of the central claim of resurrection through the empty tomb stories.

In Matthew's Gospel the good news of the resurrection is announced by an angel to "Mary Magdalene and the other Mary" (Matt 28:1) when they come to the tomb. The angel says: "Do not be afraid! I know you are seeking Jesus the crucified. He is not here, for he has been raised just as he said. Come and see the place where he lay. Then go quickly and tell his disciples, 'He has been raised from the dead, and he is going before you to Galilee; there you will see him.' Behold, I have told you" (Matt 28:5–7). This same good news is announced in Mark by a man dressed in white (Mark 16:5–7) and in Luke by "two men in dazzling garments" (Luke 24:4–6). (Remember, the word *angel* means *messenger*. In each account, the significance of the empty tomb is explained by God's messenger.)

John, as discussed in chapter 4, does not place the good news of Jesus's resurrection on the lips of an angel or a person dressed in white, but has the beloved disciple and Peter rush to the tomb after hearing from Mary Magdalene that the tomb is empty. The beloved disciple, the person who represents love, is the first to believe.

THE ACTS OF THE APOSTLES

The Acts of the Apostles also teaches the absolute centrality of Christ's resurrection. This is clear as Peter preaches to the assembled crowd on Pentecost. Peter says:

> You who are Israelites, hear these words. Jesus the Nazorean was a man commended to you by God with mighty deeds, wonders, and signs, which God worked through him in your midst, as you yourselves know. This man, delivered up by the set plan and foreknowledge of God, you killed, using lawless men to crucify him. But God raised him up, releasing him from the throes of death, because it was impossible for him to be held by it. (Acts 2:22–24)

It is because of the resurrection that the early Church began to understand Jesus's divinity and Jesus's revelatory role in the unfolding of human history. In the light of the resurrection, Peter is able to say, "Therefore let the whole house of Israel know for certain that God has made him both Lord and Messiah, this Jesus whom you crucified" (Acts 2:36).

THE LETTERS

The letters, too, insist on the fact of the resurrection as well as the centrality of this fact to the very existence of Christianity. Paul states the case most forcefully in 1 Corinthians:

> For I handed on to you as of first importance what I also received: that Christ died for our sins in accordance with the scripture; that he was buried; that he was raised on the third day in accordance with the scripture; that he appeared to Cephas, then to the Twelve. After that, he appeared to more than five hundred brothers at once, most of whom are still living, though some have fallen asleep. After that he appeared to

James, then to all the apostles. Last of all, as to one born abnor-
mally, he appeared to me. (1 Cor 15:3–8)

Paul isn't relying just on the witness of others. He knows Christ
has risen from the dead because he himself experienced the risen
Christ's presence, asking him, "Saul, Saul, why are you persecuting me" (Acts 9:4; see chapter 4). So, he can argue forcefully
against those in Corinth who don't believe in the possibility of a
resurrection from the dead. Paul says:

> But if Christ is preached as raised from the dead, how can
> some among you say there is no resurrection of the dead? If
> there is no resurrection of the dead, then neither has Christ
> been raised. And if Christ has not been raised, then empty
> [too] is our preaching; empty, too, your faith. Then we are also
> false witnesses to God, because we testified against God that
> he raised Christ, whom he did not raise if in fact the dead are
> not raised. For if the dead are not raised, neither has Christ
> been raised, and if Christ has not been raised, your faith is vain;
> you are still in your sins. Then those who have fallen asleep in
> Christ have perished. If for this life only we have hoped in
> Christ, we are the most pitiable people of all. (1 Cor 15:12–19)

The Gospels and Acts were written later than Paul's letter to
the Corinthians. From the earliest to the latest writings in the New
Testament, the resurrection is the core event upon which everything else rests. All other beliefs flow from the resurrection: our
understanding of Jesus's identity, the authority we therefore put
behind Jesus's teachings, and our own hope in life after death,
both for our loved ones and for ourselves.

THE BOOK OF REVELATION

The whole context for the book of Revelation is that Jesus has
conquered sin and death and that he already reigns victorious in
the heavenly kingdom. The setting for the book is the heavenly

kingdom. All the visions that are described proceed from the heavenly court. The lamb who is victorious is the only one worthy to open the seals that precipitate events on earth:

> Then I saw standing in the midst of the throne and the four living creatures and the elders a Lamb that seemed to have been slain . . . . He came and received the scroll from the right hand of the one who sat on the throne. When he took it . . . they sang a new hymn:

> "Worthy are you to receive the scroll and to break open its seals,
> for you were slain and with your blood you purchased for God
> those from every tribe and tongue, people and nation.
> You made them a kingdom and priests for our God,
> and they will reign on earth" (Rev 5:6, 7–8, 9–10).

To say that the lamb is the only one worthy to open the seals, thus precipitating the unfolding of events, is, through symbolic language, saying that the risen Christ, even during times of suffering and persecution, has not lost control of the course of human history.

The book of Revelation was written to people facing persecution and is exhorting them not to lose faith during their time of suffering. They, like Christ, will be victorious in the end, if not in this life, then in the next life. For this reason, the book has a strong martyrology, assuring those still suffering on earth that those who have been killed during the persecution are now victorious in heaven with Christ:

> Then one of the elders spoke up and said to me, "Who are these wearing white robes, and where did they come from?" I said to him, "My lord, you are the one who knows." He said to me, "These are the ones who have survived the time of great distress; they have washed their robes and made them white in the blood of the Lamb.

> For this reason they stand before God's throne
> and worship him day and night in his temple.

The one who sits on the throne will shelter them.
They will not hunger or thirst anymore,
nor will the sun or any heat strike them.
For the Lamb who is in the center of the throne will shepherd
them
and lead them to springs of life-giving water,
and God will wipe away every tear from their eyes." (Rev
7:13–17)

The book of Revelation, written to give hope to suffering people, places all hope in Jesus Christ, the lamb of God, and on his
resurrection, on his victory over death.

THE MYSTERY OF SUFFERING IN THE OLD TESTAMENT

To place our hope firmly in Jesus Christ, who conquered death
and still lives in our midst, certainly gives our hope a firm anchor.
However, even believing in Christ's victory, we are still confronted
with the mystery of suffering. Why do human beings suffer? What
hope is there in suffering?

As is the case in regard to every mystery that Scripture explores, the Bible models a process of coming to understanding
about the reasons for suffering. The first story that addresses the
question is the story of the man and woman in the garden (Gen
2:4–3:24). This story dates to around 1000 B.C. While many people refer to this as the second creation story, it is really not about
creation. Creation is simply an early plot element, setting the stage
for what follows. The story is responding to the question, "Why do
human beings suffer?"

The kind of suffering being discussed is that suffering known to
every generation and named near the end of the story when God
explains to the man and woman the ramifications of their choices
(see Gen 3:17–20): working by the sweat of the brow to survive,
one person's lording it over another, bearing children in pain,

dying. The plot of the story can be summarized as: There is a place of no suffering; there is an act of people's disobeying God's revealed moral order; there is a place of suffering.

The story is told through symbolic language. The man, Adam (a neuter collective noun), stands for each one of us. The woman stands for the other person whom each of us needs to be known and loved by, and to know and love. The tree of knowledge of good and evil stands for the fact that there is a moral order, a moral order that has been revealed to us by God. Some behaviors lead to life; other behaviors, such as eating the fruit of the tree of knowledge of good and evil, lead to death. The serpent stands for temptation.

Before eating of the tree of knowledge of good and evil, the man and woman do not suffer. They are in right relationship with God: They walk and talk with God every evening. They are in right relationship with each other: The man says, "This one, at last, is bone of my bones / and flesh of my flesh" (Gen 2:23). The two are like one person. The man and woman are in right relationship with themselves, symbolized by their being naked but unashamed. They are in right relationship with their world. They do not even suffer death: They can eat from the tree of life and live forever.

However, when the man and woman knowingly act contrary to the revealed moral order, when they eat the fruit of the tree of knowledge of good and evil, all of their right relationships crumble. They suffer self-alienation, being ashamed of their nakedness. They suffer separation from God, evident not because God punishes them but because they hide from God. They suffer alienation from each other: Adam blames Eve. They suffer alienation from their world. Now they must work by the sweat of the brow, and they can no longer eat from the tree of life and live forever.

This symbol story is not teaching history or biology; it is teaching theology. It is orienting us in a moral universe and teaching us that sin inevitably causes suffering because it destroys our integrity and destroys our ability to be in right relationship with God, self, others, and our world.

For many years the Israelites believed not only that sin inevitably caused suffering but that all suffering was due to sin. However, this belief began to be questioned in the sixth century B.C., during and after the Babylonian exile (587–537 B.C.). The Israelites suffered terribly at the hands of the Babylonians who destroyed their nation, destroyed their Temple, and forced the upper-class citizens to live in exile in Babylon. Why would God allow such suffering?

This question is addressed head on in the book of Job, a debate about why human beings suffer. The inspired author sets the stage by presenting us with Job, who we know is innocent because God says so, and who we know is suffering. Job's contemporaries all argue the belief of the time: Job must deserve his suffering. Job is being punished for his sins. To think otherwise was to challenge either the belief that God is all loving or the belief that God is all-powerful.

However, the author has God enter the debate and say that the friends are wrong. Job's suffering is not punishment, but it does have a purpose. However, the author does not know what the purpose is. As we have already discussed, the author of Job lived before the Israelites came to a belief in life after death, so he could not consider the problem of suffering in that broader context.

Another inspired author at the time of the Babylonian exile, called 2 Isaiah (Is 40–55), also probes the mystery of suffering. He wants to give hope to the exiles in Babylon. The hope he offers them is that their suffering is not all punishment for sin:

> Comfort, give comfort to my people,
> says your God.
> Speak tenderly to Jerusalem, and proclaim to her
> that her service is at an end,
> her guilt is expiated;
> Indeed, she has received from the hand of the Lord
> double for all her sins. (Is 40:1–2)

Rather, through their suffering, God is accomplishing something wonderful and new:

> Remember not the events of the past,
> the things of long ago consider not;
> See, I am doing something new!
> Now it springs forth, do you not perceive it?
> In the desert I make a way,
> in the wasteland, rivers. (Is 43:18–19)

We will discuss just what it is that God is accomplishing through the Israelites' suffering later in this chapter and again in chapter 7 when we trace the Israelites' expanding understanding that God is love.

THE MYSTERY OF SUFFERING IN THE NEW TESTAMENT

It is in the New Testament that we learn more about the mystery of suffering. This added insight doesn't solve the whole mystery of suffering, but it does add to our understanding. Jesus is an innocent person who suffers. So, Jesus's suffering is not punishment for personal sin. Jesus's suffering is a revelation of God's love for us and a revelation that suffering leads, not to death, but to new life. We Christians believe that if we take Jesus as our model and accept unavoidable suffering, uniting our suffering to Christ's, our suffering, too, can lead to new life both for ourselves and for others.

New Life for Ourselves

Paul, in his letter to the Romans, describes the positive effects that suffering can have in a person's life. Paul say, "Not only that, but we even boast of our afflictions, knowing that affliction produces endurance, and endurance, proven character, and proven character, hope, and hope does not disappoint, because the love of God has been poured out into our hearts through the holy Spirit that has been given us" (Rom 5:3–5). Far from being punishment, suffering is sometimes, in hindsight, seen as a gift. We recognize that because of our suffering we have become different people: more sympathetic, more understanding, stronger, more generous, and more loving.

New Life for Others

The author of Colossians (attributed to Paul but thought by many biblical scholars to have been written later, around 80 A.D.) finds meaning in his suffering by uniting it to Christ's suffering: "Now I rejoice in my sufferings for your sake, and in my flesh I am filling up what is lacking in the afflictions of Christ on behalf of his body, which is the church, of which I am a minister in accordance with God's stewardship given to me to bring to completion for you the word of God, the mystery hidden from ages and from generations past" (Col 1:24–26).

One cannot read this passage without asking, "What could possibly be 'lacking in the afflictions of Christ'?" We know from the letter to the Hebrews that Christ offered the perfect sacrifice, himself, a sacrifice that never need be repeated (see Heb 10:11–14). Still, the author of Colossians believes that he is joining Christ in his redemptive suffering, and that the author's suffering, too, will be efficacious for the Church.

One way of trying to understand how our suffering could be redemptive for other people is to compare Christ's redemptive actions with Christ's creative actions. I believe that only God can create a human being. I consider that my children belong to God before they belong to my husband and to me. At the same time, God has so arranged things that human beings are invited to participate in God's creative power. My husband and I had the privilege of doing that when we helped bring our children into the world.

In the same way, only God can redeem. However, God has arranged things so that we are privileged to share in God's redemptive power. Embracing unavoidable suffering and uniting it to Christ's suffering is the way in which we accept God's invitation to do that.

It was this idea, that through their suffering God was accomplishing something wonderful and new for other nations, which 2 Isaiah offered as hope to the exiles in Babylon. In 2 Isaiah, the nation, Israel, as God's servant, is seen as bringing other nations to a knowledge of God. In the light of the crucifixion, the early Church applied Isaiah's words to Christ. The text of 2 Isaiah pictures the kings of other nations saying:

> We had all gone astray like sheep,
> each following his own way;
> But the Lord laid upon him
> the guilt of us all.
> Though he was harshly treated he submitted
> and opened not his mouth.
> Like a lamb led to the slaughter
> or a sheep before the shearers,
> he was silent and opened not his mouth.
> Oppressed and condemned, he was taken away,
> and who would have thought any more of his destiny? . . .
> If he gives his life as an offering for sin,
> he shall see his descendants in a long life
> and the will of the Lord shall be
> accomplished through him.
> Because of his affliction,
> he shall see the light in fullness of days;
> Through his suffering, my servant shall justify many. (Is 53:6–8, 10b–11)

What was true of the exiles in Babylon and what was true for Jesus is also true for us. God can do something wonderful and new, perhaps something even beyond our imagination, through the suffering of those who join their suffering to Christ's.

AN ACCOUNT OF OUR HOPE

To believe in life after death, and to believe that suffering has a purpose in God's loving plan for God's people, either for the person suffering or for others, doesn't relieve us of the pain of suffering, but it does change our experience of suffering. It motivates us to accept suffering rather than to avoid it by acts of unfaithfulness. It fills us with purpose and a commitment to see the situation through as lovingly as possible. It leads us to model ourselves on Christ and to willingly accept suffering so as to fulfill God's loving purpose, even if that purpose is beyond our comprehension. Finally, it motivates us to model ourselves on Christ and to pray, "Not as I will, but as you will" (Mark 26:39). United to Christ's suffering, our suffering, too, can help to accomplish God's will for the world.

SPIRITUAL LESSONS LEARNED / REFLECTIONS

1. It is important to have hope and to be able to offer hope to others.

   - Am I able to give an explanation for my hope?
   - Am I able to do so with "gentleness and kindness"?

   "May the God of hope fill you with all joy and peace in believing, so that you may abound in hope by the power of the Holy Spirit" (Rom 15:13).

2. Scripture is a great source of wisdom on life's ultimate meaning and on how to live so as to be in right relationship with God and others.

   - Do I trust Scripture as a source of wisdom?
   - Do I read Scripture so as to receive that wisdom?
   - Does Scripture have authority in my life?

"Indeed, the word of God is living and effective, sharper than any two-edged sword, penetrating even between soul and spirit, joints and marrow, and able to discern reflections and thoughts of the heart" (Heb 4:12).

3. Historically, God revealed God's self through events.

- Do I believe that God still reveals God's self through events?
- Am I open to growing in my understanding of life and its meaning through probing God's ongoing self-revelation through events?

"The Lord has done great things for us" (Ps 126:3).

"How numerous have you made, / O Lord, my God, your wondrous deeds! / And in your plans for us / there is none to equal you; / Should I wish to declare or to tell them, / they would be too many to recount" (Ps 40:6).

4. There is life after death.

- What evidence does Scripture give for life after death?
- How does my belief in life after death affect my ability to cope with the death of my loved ones?
- How does my belief in life after death affect the choices I make on earth?

"Who are these wearing white robes, and where did they come from? . . .These are the ones who have survived the time of great distress; they have washed their robes and made them white in the blood of the lamb. For this reason they stand before God's throne" (Rev 7:13, 14b–15a).

5. Sin causes suffering.

- Which of my sufferings are the fruit of sin?
- What can I do to change my behavior and alleviate these sufferings?

"Do not sin anymore so that nothing worse may happen to you" (John 5:14).

6. Suffering can lead to positive personal growth.

- Am I a wiser person because of my suffering? In what way?
- Am I a stronger, more compassionate person because of my suffering? In what way?

"Consider it a joy, my brothers, when you encounter various trials, for you know that the testing of your faith produces perseverance. And let perseverance be perfect, so that you may be perfect and complete, lacking in nothing" (James 1:2–4).

7. Through my suffering God can accomplish good in the lives of others.

- Am I aware of the ways I have benefited from the sufferings of others?
- Am I aware of the ways others have benefited from my suffering?

"We know that all things work for good for those who love God, who are called according to his purpose" (Rom 8:28).

7

DISCERNING CHRIST IN ALL OF CREATION

Before my father's death I had outgrown my childhood prejudicial belief that only Roman Catholics could be saved. Due to the events surrounding his death, I gradually began to understand more clearly just how completely Jesus identifies himself with his followers and that all who are members of the body of Christ are to see Christ in each other and to be Christ for each other.

With this firm foundation, my understanding continued to broaden. Over the last twenty years, my understanding of what has been and is being accomplished through the risen Christ has expanded gradually from its effects on all Christians, to people of all world religions, to all human beings, and, finally, to all that exists. I believe that Scripture plants the seeds for people of our time in history to see the risen Christ as a cosmic Christ who has redeemed all of creation and whose offer of salvation, a shared life of love in union with God, is being accepted by people of all world religions and all nations.

By saying that "Scripture plants the seeds for people of our time in history to see the risen Christ as a cosmic Christ," I am embracing the idea that Scripture is a living word that can help people of later centuries conceptualize and name facts about our world that were completely unknown to the people who lived between 1850 B.C. and the early second century A.D., the time period that underlies the events that are pondered in Scripture.

For instance, no biblical author understood what we now understand about our earth. All biblical writers presumed that the earth had been created, not that it is being created. They presumed that the earth is flat and that heaven is up, not that the earth is round, is rotating on its own axis, and is traveling through space. As science tells us more and more about the reality of the world in which we live, we will have to reimage the spiritual truths that we are trying to understand and teach. We are in a process of becoming, and in a process of understanding, the physical world in which we live.

This process of coming to knowledge is taking place not only in the scientific realm, but in the spiritual realm. It has always been taking place. Both the Old and New Testaments model an ongoing process of revelation, one that becomes more and more expansive as people come to a deeper understanding of the ramifications of the idea that God is love. I believe that the same process of expansion in our understanding of God as love is just as necessary right now in the twenty-first century.

AN EXPANDING UNDERSTANDING OF GOD AS LOVE IN THE OLD TESTAMENT

When we read the Pentateuch (the first five books of the Old Testament) today, the story begins with God creating the world. That has been the beginning of the connected narrative that Christians call the *Old Testament* since about 450 B.C. However, if we had read the story of Israel's salvation history at the time of King David, about 1000 B.C., or any time in the following 600 years, the connected narrative about the salvation history of Israel would have begun with the story of the man and woman in the garden. This story, about the terrible consequences of sin, helped set the stage for the story of the call of Abraham, the beginning of Israel's salvation history.

For many years, the Israelites realized that God loved them, but not that God loved everyone (much like my childhood understanding that God saved Catholics, but not anyone else). This presumption is apparent in the stories the Israelites told of God's mighty acts on their behalf. For instance, in Genesis, God is pictured as telling Abraham: "I will bless those who bless you and curse those who curse you" (Gen 12:3). God is always on Israel's side, not on the side of any other nation.

This conviction that God loved the Israelites, not in addition to other nations, but before all other nations, is also evident in the story of the Israelites' moving back to the holy land after the Exodus from Egypt. God is pictured as saying, "I will have the fear of me precede you, so that I will throw into panic every nation you reach. I will make all your enemies turn from you in flight, and ahead of you I will send hornets to drive the Hivites, Canaanites and Hittites out of your way" (Ex 23:27–28). In Deuteronomy we read that when the Israelites conquered other people they were to show them no pity: "Make no covenant with them and show them no mercy. You shall not intermarry with them, neither giving your daughters to their sons nor taking their daughters for your sons. . . . For you are a people sacred to the Lord, your God; he has chosen you from all the nations on the face of the earth to be a people peculiarly his own" (Deut 7:2b–3, 6).

This understanding that God loves the Israelites, but not their enemies, is evident even in the Israelites' early prayer life. In Psalm 58, the psalmist prays for the total destruction of his enemies:

> O God, smash the teeth in their mouths;
> break the jaw-teeth of these lions, Lord!
> Make them vanish like water flowing away;
> trodden down, let them wither like grass.
> Let them dissolve like a snail that oozes away,
> like an untimely birth that never sees the sun. (Ps 58:7–9)

The Israelites did believe that God is loving. This is evident in the words of the prophet Hosea. Hosea was married to an unfaithful wife. According to the law, Hosea could have had her stoned to death. However, Hosea did not want to do that because he loved her. He wanted her to repent and return. Hosea understood his relationship with his unfaithful wife as analogous to God's situation with unfaithful Israel. God could destroy Israel, but God does not want to do that because God loves Israel. Hosea pictures God saying:

> I will espouse you to me forever;
> I will espouse you in right and in justice,
> in love and in mercy;
> I will espouse you in fidelity,
> and you shall know the Lord. (Hosea 2:21–22)

However, it is one thing to realize that God loves you. It is another thing entirely to realize that God loves other nations, even those nations that are your enemies.

The Israelites came to the understanding that God loved other nations in addition to themselves by reflecting on experience. The first experience was the Babylonian exile (587–537 B.C.). A prophet to the exiles, 2 Isaiah tried to help the Israelites make sense out of the fact that their nation and temple had been destroyed and they were now in exile in Babylon (Is 40–55). As we mentioned in chapter 6, the hope that 2 Isaiah offered the exiles was that God was accomplishing something wonderful through them. Through their sufferings they would bring other nations to a knowledge of God. The prophet 2 Isaiah pictures the rulers of other nations saying:

> We had all gone astray like sheep,
> each following his own way;
> But the Lord laid upon him
> the guilt of us all. (Is 53:6)

Then God, referring to Israel as God's servant, says: "Through his suffering, my servant shall justify many" (Is 53:11b). Through Israel's suffering God was drawing other nations to God's self just as God had drawn Israel to God's self. Therefore, God must love these other nations.

The second experience was the way in which the exile ended. Cyrus, who was a Persian, conquered the Babylonians and allowed the Israelites to return home. The Israelites reasoned that if God could use a Persian as the instrument of God's saving power, God must love Persians. In fact, Cyrus was understood by the Israelites to be a *messiah*, an *anointed one*.

> Thus says the Lord to his anointed, Cyrus
> whose right hand I grasp,
> Subduing nations before him,
> and making kings run in his service. . . .
> I will give you treasures out of the darkness,
> and riches that have been hidden away,
> That you may know that I am the Lord
> the God of Israel, who calls you by your name. (Is 45:1, 3)

Persia was among the nations whom God was calling to God's self.

In the light of these experiences, one inspired author wrote a humorous story to teach an unwelcome message: God loves even our enemies. This truth is being taught through the story of Jonah. While the author lived about 450 B.C., the story is set some 300 years earlier when Assyria was the nation threatening Israel. It was Assyria that conquered the ten northern tribes, often called the lost tribes of Israel. Nineveh was the capital of Assyria.

The author of Jonah pictures God telling Jonah to preach to the Ninevites. Jonah doesn't want to do it. Nineveh is the enemy, and Jonah doesn't want them saved. However, after being swallowed by a fish, undergoing a conversion of heart, and being vomited up by the fish, Jonah does preach to the Ninevites. He only has to say one sentence, "Forty days more and Nineveh will be destroyed" (Jonah 3:4), and everyone converts: the king, the people, even the cows wear sack cloth and ashes. Since the people had repented, God decides not to destroy them after all.

Jonah is furious. God, of course, still loves Jonah, so God asks Jonah if he has a reason to be so angry. Jonah feels fully justified in his anger: God wasn't going to destroy the Ninevites after all, and, besides that, Jonah is hot because the plant that had given him shade had been withered by a worm. God points out to Jonah that he did not labor over or raise the shade plant. On the other hand, God did labor over and raise the Ninevites. Of course God is concerned for the Ninevites and does not want to destroy them.

Although the author of Jonah leavens his message with humor, the message itself is hard to swallow. The idea that God loves other nations, too, has profound ramifications in the way Israel interacts with other nations. Other nations, too, are beloved children of God.

It is at this time, after the Babylonian exile, and after the Israelites have come to an understanding that God made all people so God must love all people that the returned exiles, under the leadership of the priests, prefaced the already existing narrative of their people with the story of God creating the whole world in six days. In that story, human beings are made in God's own image, and God says that all that God has created is very good (Gen 1:1–2:4). By prefacing the story of salvation history with this story, the priestly editors universalized all that follows. The story of the call of Abraham is no longer just the story of Israel's salvation history, but of the whole world's salvation history. God's intent is to call all nations to a knowledge of their God.

AN EXPANDING UNDERSTANDING OF GOD AS LOVE IN THE NEW TESTAMENT

The New Testament, too, models an expanding understanding of the ramifications of the fact that God is love. In Matthew's Gospel, when Jesus is pictured giving instructions to the Apostles, he says, "Do not go into pagan territory or enter a Samaritan town. Go rather to the lost sheep of the house of Israel" (Matt 10:5–6).

One of the most puzzling passages in Matthew seems to be understandable only in this context. A Canaanite woman asks Jesus to heal her daughter. Matthew tells us that Jesus "did not say a word in answer to her. His disciples came and asked him, 'Send her away, for she keeps calling out after us,' He said in reply, 'I was sent only to the lost sheep of the house of Israel. . . . It is not right to take the food of the children and throw it to the dogs'" (Matt 15:23–24, 26). The woman is not insulted or discouraged. She engages Jesus in a witty and persuasive reply. In response, Jesus says, "O woman, great is your faith! Let it be done for you as you wish" (Matt 15:28).

It seems that Jesus initially instructed his disciples to go only to their fellow Jews. That is why they felt free to ignore the woman's need and send her away. However, in response to the woman's faith and persistence, Jesus disobeyed his own instructions and responded to the woman's need.

It is clear in the Acts of the Apostles that Peter did not understand until well after the resurrection that Jesus's mission was now to include the Gentiles. Peter has a dream in which a sheet full of clean and unclean animals was lowered before him. A voice said to Peter, "'Slaughter and eat.' But Peter said, 'Certainly not, sir. For never have I eaten anything profane and unclean.' The voice spoke to him again, a second time, 'What God has made clean, you are not to call profane'" (Acts 10:13–15).

It is only because Peter had this dream that he agreed to go to Cornelius's house. Otherwise, he would have called Cornelius's house unclean, since Cornelius was a Gentile. Once there, he saw that the Gentiles had already received the Holy Spirit. Peter then said, "In truth, I see that God shows no partiality. Rather, in every nation whoever fears him and acts uprightly is acceptable to him" (Acts 10:34–35).

This insight is a huge breakthrough for Peter and for the first century Church. God has no partiality among nations. God made all people, and God loves all people. This broader understanding of the Church's role appears in the commissioning in Matthew's Gospel. Jesus commissions the disciples to "make disciples of all nations, baptizing them in the name of the Father, and of the Son, and of the holy Spirit" (Matt 28:19).

Once other nations come to know Israel's God, do the other nations have to relate to God just as the Jews do? Must they obey the Jewish law? Must they be circumcised? As Acts tell us, some were saying, "Unless you are circumcised according to the Mosaic practice, you cannot be saved" (Acts 15:1). This dilemma was the subject of discussion at the first Church council, the Jerusalem Council. Under the inspiration of the Spirit, and based on a process of group discernment, the Church decided that Gentiles would not have to become Jews in order to become Christians. Peter gave witness to his experience, saying, "God, who knows the heart, bore witness by granting them [i.e. the Gentiles in Cornelius's house] the holy Spirit just as he did us. He made no distinction between us and them, for by faith he purified their hearts . . . . We believe that we are saved through the grace of the Lord Jesus, in the same way as they" (Acts 15:8–9, 11). The Church then promulgated this new and revolutionary teaching. All people are invited into covenant love with God.

AN EXPANDING UNDERSTANDING OF GOD AS LOVE IN THE TWENTY-FIRST CENTURY

Just as I, as a young Catholic, believed that only Catholics could be saved, so do many Christians believe that only Christians can be saved. They quote a variety of passages from Scripture to prove their point: For instance, in Mark's Gospel, Jesus is pictured as saying, "Whoever believes and is baptized will be saved; whoever does not believe will be condemned" (Mark 16:16). In his letter to the Romans, Paul says: "If you confess with your mouth that Jesus is Lord and believe in your heart that God raised him from the dead, you will be saved. For one believes with the heart and so is justified, and one confesses with the mouth and so is saved" (Rom 10:9–10). In John's Gospel Jesus says, "I am the gate. Whoever enters through me will be saved" (John 10:9). Do these passages teach that unless a person is self-consciously Christian, that person cannot be saved?

If we interpret the passages that way, we would have trouble explaining Matthew's parable of the judgment of the nations (Matt

25:31–46). As we pointed out in chapter 4, in this parable Jesus teaches that the way we treat the marginalized is the way we are treating Jesus himself. In the parable, the people who have fed the hungry and clothed the naked ask, "'Lord, when was it that we saw you hungry and gave you food, or thirsty and gave you something to drink? And when was it that we saw you a stranger and welcomed you, or naked and gave you clothing? And when was it that we saw you sick or in prison and visited you?' And the king will answer them, 'Truly I tell you, just as you did it to one of the least of these who are members of my family, you did it to me'" (Matt 25:37b–40; NRSV). It is those who acted lovingly, not knowing that in doing so they were serving their king, who will "inherit the kingdom" (Matt 25:34).

Does this passage from Matthew contradict the passages just quoted from Mark, Romans, and John? It does not. When we place the passages from Mark, Romans, and John in the context in which each appears in the Bible, we see that none of them is addressing the question we are asking: Can only those who know Christ be saved by Christ? Mark is teaching that those to whom the good news of Jesus Christ is revealed, and who actively reject it, will not be saved. Paul is teaching that both Jews and Gentiles are saved through faith, not through obedience to the law. John is teaching that Jesus, unlike the Pharisees with whom Jesus is arguing, is the good shepherd who is leading his sheep to the Father. The Pharisees are blocking people's way to God by their legalistic teachings. None of these passages is addressing the question: Can sincere truth seekers who do not know Christ be saved?

Since Vatican Council II, it has been the teaching of the Catholic Church that the answer to this question is yes. This belief is stated in the Vatican II Document, *Pastoral Constitution on the Church in the Modern World* (*Gaudium et Spes*, 1965) which says: "Since Christ died for all, and since all men are in fact called to one and the same destiny, which is divine, we must hold that the Holy Spirit offers to all the possibility of being made partners, in a way known to God, of the Paschal mystery" (*Gaudium et Spes* 22 par. 5). Quoting this statement, the *Catechism of the Catholic*

Church goes on to say, "Every man who is ignorant of the Gospel of Christ and his Church, but seeks the truth and does the will of God in accordance with his understanding of it, can be saved" (*Catechism of the Catholic Church* par. 1260).

However, the *Catechism* seems to be ambivalent on this matter. In an earlier paragraph, addressing the question of the necessity of faith, the *Catechism* says:

> Believing in Jesus Christ and in the One who sent him for our salvation is necessary for obtaining that salvation. "Since 'without faith it is impossible to please [God]' and to attain to the fellowship of his sons, therefore without faith no one has ever attained justification, nor will anyone obtain eternal life 'but he who endures to the end.'" (*Catechism of the Catholic Church* par. 161)

It appears that the present-day Church is undergoing the same kind of expansion in understanding the ramifications of the fact that God is love that our ancestors in faith in both the Old and New Testaments underwent. However, I think the seeds for this broader understanding are present in Scripture. Building on Scripture, one can, through reason, reach the conclusion that God loves and offers salvation to all sincere truth seekers, not just to those who have embraced Christianity.

GOD IS LOVE

The author of 1 John states the core revelation of the Gospels very clearly. He writes:

> Beloved, let us love one another, because love is of God; everyone who loves is begotten by God and knows God. Whoever is without love does not know God, for God is love. In this way the love of God was revealed to us: God sent his only Son into the world so that we might have life through him. In this is love: not that we have loved God, but that he loved us and sent

his Son as expiation for our sins. . . . If we love one another,
God remains in us, and his love is brought to perfection in us.
(1 John 4:7–10, 12)

God is love. If we keep this truth uppermost in our thinking,
the universal and ever-persistent nature of God's love becomes
self-evident. Starting with the insight of the Israelites after the
Babylonian exile, we can conclude that because God created all
people, God must love all people. Why would a loving God create
all people but redeem only some people? The author of 1 John
assures us that this is not the case: "[Jesus] is expiation for our sins,
and not for our sins only but for those of the whole world" (1 John
2:2).

The whole world has been redeemed, that is, freed from slavery to sin. Does that mean that the whole world is saved? Certainly
salvation is offered to all. However, whether or not a person experiences the gifts that he or she has received through Jesus Christ
depends on whether or not that person accepts those gifts. A person who is sincerely seeking the truth and is growing in love has
accepted those gifts. The source of love is God. To love is to
participate in God's life. Christians believe that Christ is the Word
of God who became flesh, is one with God, is God (John 1: 1).
Therefore, a loving person who does not consciously know Christ
is still united to Christ precisely because that loving person is
united to God.

We can arrive at the same conclusion by thinking about the fact
that Jesus continually referred to God as his father, a loving parent. What loving parent would choose among his or her children,
acting for one's good but for another's ruin? Certainly, we human
beings are not more loving than God. Jesus draws this very comparison between his heavenly Father and human parents when he
says, "Which one of you would hand his son a stone when he asks
for a loaf of bread, or a snake when he asks for a fish? If you then,
who are wicked, know how to give good gifts to your children, how
much more will your heavenly Father give good things to those
who ask him" (Matt 7:9–11). It is God's will to save all of God's

beloved children. Those who seek God will find God, if not in identical creeds, in loving relationships. Where there is love, there is God.

THE COSMIC CHRIST

In the Acts of the Apostles, when Peter is speaking before the Sanhedrin and is asked by what power or by what name he had healed a crippled beggar, Peter responds that it was in "the name of Jesus Christ, the Nazorean." Peter goes on to say: "There is no salvation through anyone else, nor is there any other name under heaven given to the human race by which we are to be saved" (Acts 4:10, 12). Given this statement, how can a person who accepts the authority of Scripture come to the conclusion that I just proposed, that loving truth seekers who do not know Christ can be saved?

I believe the seeds for such a belief can be found in John's Gospel. Remember, based on the experience I had when my father was dying, the refrain that I have constantly running in my mind is, "I don't think you recognized me." So, as I read biblical texts and live my everyday life, I am asking myself, "How is God making God's self present right now? Am I still failing to recognize God's presence?"

As I read and thought about John's gospel, especially the prologue and the I AM statements, I began to realize that John's Gospel impregnates all of creation with the presence of God. As John explains it, everything that exists exists in and through God's Word, a Word that became flesh and dwelt among us. The Gospel begins:

> In the beginning was the Word,
> And the Word was with God,
> And the Word was God.
> All things came to be through him,
> and without him nothing came to be.
> What came to be through him was life,

And this life was the light of the human race;
The light shines in the darkness,
And the darkness has not overcome it. . . .
He was in the world,
And the world came to be through him,
but the world did not know him. (John 1:1–5, 10)

Notice that this high Christology hymn (*high Christology* means that it emphasizes Christ's divinity) begins with the exact same words with which the book of Genesis begins: "In the beginning." The author of John is purposefully alluding to the book of Genesis, and will continue to do that. Both books begin before creation. In the Genesis story, God creates by speaking. God says, "Let there be . . ." and that creation comes into existence. In John, that speaking, that Word becomes a person who is both with God and is God. All that exists exists in and through that Word. All that is alive is sharing in the life of the creative Word of God.

John then tells us that this "Word became flesh / and made his dwelling among us . . ." (John 1:14a). As we noted in chapter 4 when discussing John's audience and theme, John is writing for late-first-century Christians who are looking for the return of the risen Christ. John wants to teach his readers that the risen Christ did return, his postresurrection appearances were a return, and Christ has never left. Christ is alive and is in their midst. One way in which John teaches this lesson is through Jesus's I AM statements.

In John's Gospel, Jesus's I AM statements are part of John's high Christology. Through these statements, John is claiming that Jesus is God. Two examples will make this point clear. When Jesus is arguing with his adversaries, Jesus says, "'Abraham your father rejoiced to see my day; he saw it and was glad.' So the Jews said to him, 'You are not yet fifty years old and you have seen Abraham?' Jesus said to them, 'Amen, amen, I say to you, before Abraham came to be, I AM'" (John 8:56–58).

For Jesus to identify himself as I AM is for Jesus to claim to be God. I AM is the name that God revealed as God's own in the story of Moses and the burning bush (Ex 3:4–22). When God calls

Moses to lead the Israelites out of slavery in Egypt, Moses replies with objections and questions. One question is, "'When I go to the Israelites and say to them, "The God of your fathers has sent me to you," if they ask me, "What is his name?" what am I to tell them?' God replied, 'I am who am.' Then he added, 'This is what you shall tell the Israelites: I AM sent me to you'" (Ex 3:13–14).

Scripture scholars debate what God is revealing about God's self by the name I AM. The Hebrew word is a first-person form of the verb "to be." Three possible meanings are: I cause to be all that exists; I cause to be all that happens; I am always with you. One need not choose among these meanings. The name could be multivalent, including all of these meanings and more.

There can be no doubt that John intends Jesus's I AM statements to be claims that Jesus is God. We can tell this by the way people around Jesus react to his words. In John 8, when Jesus claims to be I AM, his adversaries are so enraged they pick up stones to throw at him (John 8:58–59).

A second example in which John makes clear his intent to claim Jesus's identity through Jesus's I AM statements is in the arrest scene. As the soldiers come to arrest Jesus, Jesus approaches them and says: "'Whom are you looking for?' They answered him, 'Jesus the Nazorean.' He said to them, 'I AM.' Judas his betrayer was also with them. When he said to them 'I AM,' they turned away and fell to the ground" (John 18:4–6). John pictures the arresting soldiers falling flat on their faces in the presence of divinity.

John gives us just this flash picture of the soldiers responding to divinity, and then the story goes on as if this had not happened. The soldiers continue to arrest Jesus. However, through Jesus's words and the other characters' reactions to Jesus's words, John has clearly taught the reader that Jesus is I AM. Jesus is God.

Through additional I AM statements, John identifies Jesus with all that is life-giving. Jesus says, "I am the bread of life" (6:35); "I am the light of the world" (8:12); "I am the way, the truth and the life" (14:6); "I am the true vine" (15:1). John impregnates all of creation with the presence of I AM, the presence of God, the presence of the Word who became flesh, the presence of the risen Christ. Christ and God are one.

So, based on the Gospel According to John and 1 John, I think one can reasonably conclude that any person who exists was created by a God who loves that person, even if the person is an atheist, and any person who is redeemed is redeemed by Jesus Christ, who is God, even if that person doesn't know Jesus Christ.

So, Peter's claim in Acts, that "there is no salvation through anyone else [i.e. anyone but Jesus], nor is there any other name under heaven given to the human race by which we are to be saved" (Acts 4:10, 12), is not precluding a belief that loving people who are not Christian are being saved. Anyone who is alive is alive through the creative Word of God. Anyone who is redeemed is redeemed through the redeeming Word of God. All who are learning how to love are accepting the gifts from the breath, the Spirit, of that Word of God. Christians are not the exclusive recipients of God's saving power any more than Christians are the exclusive recipients of life, of light, of the crops of the earth that we form into bread, of truth that has been revealed by God, or of knowledge about the way to live so as to please God.

ONE GOD OF ALL

Sometimes Christians think that those who belong to other world religions worship a different God than do Christians, a false god. This is not the case. There is only one God to worship. All who are praying are praying to that one God. So, no matter what we call that God, we are all still praying to the same God. The fact that my understanding of God is Trinitarian, Father, Son, and Holy Spirit, does not mean that I know a different God. It only means that I know the one God differently.

When teaching about God and God's kingdom, as those of us who teach Scripture are doing, we must understand and acknowledge that God and God's kingdom are beyond our comprehension. So, everything we say about God and the kingdom is inadequate in expressing the truth and uses metaphorical language. For instance, we compare God, who is beyond our understanding, to aspects of God that are within our understanding. That is, if I say, "God is my rock," I am not equating God with a rock, but I am saying that God and a rock have something in common: God gives me stability; God is my firm foundation. I am not saying that God is hard and unfeeling. A variety of metaphors cast light on various aspects of God.

In addition, the fact that we call God different names does not mean that we are believing in different gods. An analogy will help make this point clear. Each of us is called by different names by those with whom we have close relationships. My birth family calls me *Margaret*. My husband and friends call me *Margie*. My children call me *Mom*. My grandchildren call me *Grandma*. My children's friends call me Mrs. Ralph. My students call me *Dr. Ralph*. No matter what name I am called, the same person is being addressed.

Even though the person my parents know (not past tense because I believe in life after death), the person my husband knows, the person each of my children knows, the person each of my grandchildren knows, the person various friends know, and the person each of my students knows are all very different, still those understandings are about the same person. To some degree, they are all true. Some have a deeper understanding than others. None of them understands everything. Each could learn from the other.

Certainly, if that is true about one person knowing another, it is true about any person or group of people knowing God. No world religion understands everything, and each of us has something to learn from the other. True, Christians believe that the fullness of revelation is in Jesus Christ. However, that does not mean that we Christians have completely understood that fullness of revelation. We, too, have more to learn.

The Christian Trinitarian concept of God lends itself to an understanding of a cosmic Christ present to and effective in all of creation, not just in the life of Christians. An analogy for the Trinity that I have found most helpful in probing this idea is this: In our solar system, there is one sun (one God). However, we experience that sun not just as existing in its own right, other than us, in the heavens (the Father). We also experience the sun as light (the Son; "I am the light of the world"), and as warmth (the Spirit who enters us; the warmth of fire; a column of fire at night during the Exodus; tongues of fire at Pentecost, something that actually enters us and enables us to flourish).

Whether or not a person shares a Christian understanding of this God who is beyond our comprehension, that person is living in intimate relationship with the one God by virtue of the fact that he or she exists, just as each of us lives not only in the presence of the sun, but benefitting from the gifts of the sun. If a person is trying to grow in love, he or she is accepting God's grace.

A VISION OF THE HEAVENLY COURT

The book of Revelation has a scene that is set in the heavenly court:

> After this I had a vision of a great multitude, which no one could count, from every nation, race, people, and tongue. They stood before the throne and before the Lamb, wearing white robes and holding palm branches in their hands. They cried out in a loud voice: "Salvation comes from our God, who is seated on the throne, / and from the Lamb." All the angels stood around the throne and around the elders and the four living creatures. They prostrated themselves before the throne, worshiped God, and exclaimed: "Amen. Blessing and glory, wisdom and thanksgiving, / honor, power and might / be to our God forever and ever. Amen." (Rev 7:9–12)

This passage comes immediately after the passage about the 144,000 sealed: "Do not damage the land or the sea or the trees until we put the seal on the foreheads of the servants of our God. I heard the number of those who had been marked with the seal, one hundred and forty-four thousand marked from every tribe of

Israel" (Rev 7:3–4). Some think that the 144,000 sealed passage as teaching that only 144,000 will be in heaven. This is a misinterpretation. Numbers in the book of Revelation are symbolic. 144,000 is 12 (12 tribes) x 12 (12 apostles) x 1,000 (wholeness). It represents the fact that there is room in heaven for everyone. The passage that follows, quoted above, pictures people from every nation, race, people, and tongue. They are all in the heavenly court. Why? Because they have been loving, faithful people on earth.

The good news of the Gospel is that Jesus has redeemed the whole world. As a Christian, I think that many loving people, as they enter the "heavenly court," will be welcomed by the Lamb with the words, "I don't think you recognized me."

SPIRITUAL LESSONS LEARNED / REFLECTIONS

1. Human beings are involved in an ongoing process of understanding both our physical and our spiritual worlds.

   - How has my understanding of our spiritual world grown and changed?
   - What could I do to continue this growth process?

   "It is not that I have already . . . attained perfect maturity, but I continue my pursuit in hope that I may possess it, since I have indeed been taken possession of by Christ [Jesus]" (Phil 3:12).

2. God created everyone and loves everyone.

   - Do I really believe that God loves everyone? Even my enemies? Even those against whom I hold some grudge?
   - What are the ramifications of this belief for the way I treat those with whom I disagree?
   - What are the ramifications of this belief for the way I regard those of other world religions?

- What are the ramifications of this belief for the way I regard the whole human race?
- Do I give witness to others of God's love for them by the way I treat them?

"Beloved, let us love one another, because love is of God; everyone who loves is begotten by God and knows God. Whoever is without love does not know God, for God is love" (1 John 4:7–8).

3. God is present in God's creation.

- What are the ramifications of this belief for the way I treat the environment?
- In what routines of my daily life might I hear the creator Word of God say to me, "I don't think you recognized me"? When I see light? When I eat bread? When I drink water?

"The heavens declare the glory of God; the sky proclaims its builder's craft" (Ps 19:2). "In the beginning was the Word, and the Word was with God, and the Word was God. He was in the beginning with God. All things came to be through him, and without him nothing came to be" (John 1:1–3). "I am the light of the world" (John 8:12); "I am the bread of life" (John 6:35).

4. Everything I know and say about God and about the kingdom of God is inadequate to the truth and uses metaphorical language.

- How do I describe God?
- In doing this, to what am I comparing God?
- What about this comparison is accurate? What is inaccurate?

"O Lord, my God, you are great indeed! / You are clothed with majesty and glory, / robed in light as with a cloak" (Ps

104:1b–2a). "[Jesus] said, 'To what shall we compare the kingdom of God, or what parable can we use for it? It is like a mustard seed'" (Mark 4:30–31a).

5. There is room in heaven for everyone.

- Do I think this is good news? Do I want everyone to be invited to the kingdom?
- While I am still on earth, in what ways might Jesus be saying to me, "I don't think you recognized me"?

"After this I had a vision of a great multitude, which no one could count, from every nation, race, people, and tongue. They stood before the throne and before the Lamb, wearing white robes and holding palm branches in their hands. They cried out in a loud voice: 'Salvation comes from our God, who is seated on the throne / and from the Lamb'" (Rev 7:9–10).

8

TWENTY YEARS LATER: SPIRITUAL AND BIBLICAL LESSONS LEARNED

I find it quite a sobering thought to realize that my husband and I are now older than my parents were when they moved to Lexington to be near our family after my father's first stroke. Instead of being the middle-aged mother of four young children and the daughter of aging parents, I am the aging parent, the mother of middle-aged children, and the grandmother of fourteen, including young adults. With age we get perspective. More and more, we see a larger picture.

I consider it one of the greatest privileges of my life that my parents moved to Lexington during their last years on earth and that I was able to accompany each of them, as first my father, and then my mother, approached the veil and moved on. As I reflect on this privilege many years later, I realize that the experiences I had with my parents as they were dying had a profound effect on my own spiritual life, on my understanding of how to be a loving wife and mother, and on my ability to be a catechist and a teacher of religious education. In this concluding chapter I am going to try to integrate the lessons, rooted in the unusual events that surrounded my father's death, I have learned over the past twenty years.

LOVE AND SUFFERING

I have come to believe that a person cannot love and, at the same time, avoid suffering. This is a mystery, a mystery that we Christians call the *mystery of the cross*, a mystery we explored in chapter 6.

When we suffer as a consequence of love rather than as a consequence of sin, as we do when our loved ones precede us in moving beyond the veil, we are entering a transformative process that will result in new life for them, for ourselves, and for others. This is the kind of unavoidable suffering that we must embrace, as Christ embraced the cross. This kind of suffering, mysteriously, appears to be part of the order of creation, part of our becoming.

While the Christian story does not tell us why suffering is part of the order of becoming, it does affirm the truth of this insight. In the letter to the Hebrews, the author, in the context of claiming that Jesus is the perfect high priest and the perfect offering, says that Jesus was perfected through suffering: "For it was fitting that he, for whom and through whom all things exist, in bringing many children to glory, should make the leader to their salvation perfect through suffering" (Heb 2:10). Later Hebrews says: "Son though he was, he learned obedience from what he suffered; and when he was made perfect, he became the source of eternal salvation for all who obey him" (Heb 5:8–9).

On first reading, these are puzzling passages because we think of Jesus as having always been perfect in the sense that Jesus did not sin. However, Jesus was human, and so he had to grow and to learn things, just as we do. Luke refers to this truth as he concludes the story of Jesus's being lost for three days in the Temple: "And Jesus advanced [in] wisdom and age and favor before God and man" (Luke 2:52). It is in this sense, in the sense of growing and learning, that Jesus is perfected through suffering. So are we.

Paul was able to rejoice in the midst of his sufferings. Writing from prison, he assures the Philippians that God is accomplishing great things through his imprisonment:

> I want you to know, beloved, that what has happened to me has actually helped to spread the gospel, so that it has become known throughout the whole imperial guard and to everyone else that my imprisonment is for Christ; and most of the brothers and sisters, having been made confident in the Lord by my imprisonment, dare to speak the word with greater boldness and without fear. (Phil 1:12–14)

Despite his suffering, Paul urges the Philippians to be joyful: "Rejoice in the Lord always; again I will say, Rejoice . . . the Lord is near. Do not worry about anything" (Phil 4:4,5b–6a).

I think my father learned this valuable lesson from his mother. I remember on one occasion, when I was going through something very difficult, my father told me that his mother used to say, "Never deprive your children of their suffering." On first glance, this sounds like terrible advice. What parent doesn't want to spare his or her children suffering? However, on closer inspection, I think there is wisdom in this advice. Sometimes each of us must travel through suffering in order to reach new life. Each of us must do it ourselves. No one can do it for us.

LIFE DOES NOT END WITH LIFE ON EARTH

We have already discussed that central to the whole New Testament is the claim that Jesus rose from the dead. Obviously, the whole idea that Christ is alive and dwells in our midst depends on the resurrection. Many Christians believe in life after death based on the witness of the Church, the witness of their ancestors in faith going back to the apostles. However, it is also true that the belief of many people in life after death rests not only on the apostolic witness, but on their own personal experiences. They have been in the presence of loved ones who are no longer living on earth.

I personally know of five people who have had such encounters. They are not extremely unusual. However, I think many people are hesitant to talk about these experiences because the experiences are precious beyond words, and it is painful to have others dismiss a deeply held conviction that a person has risked sharing. They don't want others to think they are weird or are losing their grip on reality. A biblical expression for sharing something precious and deeply spiritual, only to have it belittled or dismissed is to "throw your pearls before swine." Matthew's Gospel pictures Jesus warning people not to do it: "Do not give what is holy to dogs, or throw your pearls before swine, lest they trample them underfoot, and turn and tear you to pieces" (Matt 7:6).

I recounted one of these life-after-death experiences in chapter 5. In that case, reconciliation was sorely needed between a mother and a daughter. Two people, the daughter and her son, experienced the presence of the mother/grandmother, so each could affirm for the other the reality of what had occurred.

Two other people, a husband and wife, had a life-after-death experience one evening when they were sitting in their family room watching TV. The husband's brother was missing. He had been boating on the Chesapeake Bay, and had not been heard from since. Suddenly the missing man appeared in the room, told them that he had drowned, and begged them to raise his daughter as though she were their own. The couple did as they were asked, welcoming the child into their home.

Another instance of a life-after-death experience occurred between a son and his father. The father was a scientist and was learning things that challenged his son's understanding of some doctrinal issues. The son was a young priest. As the priest described it years later, as a youth he had been arrogant in his convictions, an attitude that resulted in some estrangement between his father and him. The father died very suddenly, before the relationship had been healed. The son suffered terribly, not just from the loss of his father, but from the fact of the estrangement. One night he saw his father at the foot of his bed. The father told him that he was fine, all was forgiven, and he did not want him to suffer any more about this. From that day on the son was able to forgive himself and move on.

In a fourth example, I did not talk with the person who had had the experience, but to her concerned mother. A mother told me that her daughter claimed that her recently deceased grandmother had appeared to her. The granddaughter was playing tennis in a championship game and serving for the possibly winning point. She was extremely nervous. She looked up in the stands and saw her grandmother. She bounced the ball, looked again, and her grandmother said, "You can do it!" She served the ball for the winning point. The mother told me this because she was trying to figure out the best way to be of loving support for her daughter. She asked me if I thought she should get her daughter some help.

I told the woman that I do not discount the reality of such experiences, and told her about other instances of like occurrences that I have described here. I also commented that, being married to a psychologist, I wouldn't hesitate to get a child help during an emotionally difficult time, but I would be extremely careful not to say anything to her daughter that reflected doubt on her part about something so precious and real to her daughter.

If one believes that Jesus rose from the dead, that his followers knew this because they experienced his presence, and that we, too, have life after death, then stories like this are completely believable, especially when you hear them from people who are describing their own experiences and are trying to come to terms with them. If one believes in life after death, one believes that relationships with loved ones do not end when a loved one no longer lives on earth. While I certainly miss not being able to have a face to face conversation with my parents, I still feel their presence more than I feel their absence. I still know that they love me and that their love is living and active in my life.

DO NOT CLING TO ME

As we discussed in chapter 4, when Jesus appeared to Mary Magdalene, she clung to him. Jesus tells her not to hold on to him because he has not yet ascended to the Father (John 20:17). Both my father and my mother lived to a ripe old age, and their deaths were gradual, not sudden. A great deal of the grieving took place before their actual deaths. So, I was not clinging to them. I had accepted that they must be free to move on.

However, in the years that followed, as I pondered all that had happened in my heart, I realized that this idea of not clinging to those we love is just as important in regard to the way we treat our loved ones on earth as it is to the way we treat our loved ones as they approach death. If we love people, we must give them the freedom to become the people God is calling them to be. We must realize that each person is uniquely made in the image of God, not in our own image.

Luke pictures Mary and Joseph learning this lesson when Jesus is twelve. After being in Jerusalem for the feast of Passover, the parents start home, not realizing that Jesus is not in the caravan. When they discover his absence, they return to Jerusalem to look for him, finally finding him in the Temple. Mary asks Jesus why he caused them so much anxiety. Jesus replies, "Did you not know that I must be in my Father's house?" (Luke 2:49).

Jesus is telling his parents that he must pursue his vocation, a vocation that will result in some degree of separation from his parents. This separation between parent and child was true between my parents and me. I married, moved away, and they had to move to Lexington for us to be together. In turn, I must leave my children completely free to go about their vocations, no matter what separations that causes.

My parents gave each other the freedom to "be in [their] Father's house." Each was free to worship God as that person felt called. Their bond of unity was love, not agreement. They also refrained from clinging to their daughters. We were each completely free to pursue our own vocations, marry those we loved, live where our responsibilities took us, and become the people we felt called to be.

Each person—our parents, our spouse, our children, our beloved friends, even ourselves—ultimately belongs to God, and we must never cling to another in a way that makes more difficult that person's becoming the person God is calling him or her to be.

LOVE AND FORGIVENESS

In chapter 6 we discussed in depth the process reflected in both the Old and New Testaments of God's people coming to understand the ramifications of the fact that God is Love. In the gospels, Jesus models the way one must act in order to be a faithful witness of God's love to others. Because God created all, loves all, and offers forgiveness and redemption to all, we must see the Word made flesh in all and be a witness of God's forgiving love to all with whom we come in contact.

This requirement that we love and forgive is not limited to family, neighborhood, or church. It crosses all boundaries: class boundaries, national boundaries, racial boundaries, and religious boundaries. Love binds people together in greater and greater unity. A person who uses biblical categories of thought might describe this intended union as becoming one body of Christ. A person who uses scientific categories of thought might describe it as becoming one organism in an ever-forming and more complex universe.

I think some of the seeds for the ideas expressed above were planted when I was in college. Remember, at that time I still thought that only Catholics could be saved. After reading a book by Pierre Teilhard de Chardin, called *The Divine Milieu*, I was very excited by the idea that we humans are part of a much bigger whole and are in the process of becoming. After reading the book, I came away with the idea that we are all in the process of being formed into a single organism, and that technology is becoming the central nervous system of that organism. I remember clearly that when President Kennedy was assassinated I thought, "This is the first time I have experienced a worldwide oneness." That was the first time I was aware of the whole world reacting at the same time to a single event because technology could inform the world of that event immediately.

Slowly, over the years, the ramifications of the idea of oneness have grown and grown. If we are called to be one, certainly Christians should not be excluding each other, as I believed was right until my late twenties. Beginning to understand and believe that my parents actually belonged to the same Church was a huge breakthrough for me. Outgrowing a well-taught and deep-seeded prejudice opened the door for me to outgrow other prejudices that cause division, that disrupt the oneness to which we are called.

If the whole human race is called to be one, Christians should not judge and look down on other world religions. After all, those who belong to other world religions are also beloved children of God. If I had been born into one of those world religions, I would probably have studied and tried to be faithful to that religion, just as I have studied and tried to be faithful to the Christian religion. Each world religion has gifts to offer the others.

If the world community is called to be one, nationalism needs to center around treasuring the unique self-identity and gifts of our particular nation for the world community, not center around proving that we are number one, superior to all others. Class divisions and racial divisions also need to be overcome. We need to learn to love and appreciate each other.

If the oneness toward which we are evolving is to be achieved, we humans need to learn to love and forgive. Forgiveness is always necessary because none of us is perfect. Once forgiveness is offered and received, we are even more free to love. Love is the bond of unity. My parents taught me that. The more we love, the more we become who we are called to be.

IN CHRIST'S NAME WE PRAY

The idea that we are called to be one has many practical implications. One example is how people of different world religions might pray together at public events. As a Christian I often end a prayer with, "In Christ's name we pray," or, "I ask this in Jesus's name." However, if I am praying in a setting where others may not be Christian, so may not be able to say "Amen" to that part of the prayer, I conclude with, "We ask this, trusting in your love and presence and knowing that you hear our prayer." Is that a cop out? As a Christian, should I insist on specifically naming Christ? I am not speaking here of an interreligious dialogue where the whole purpose is to give individual witness to our specific expressions of faith. I'm speaking of an occasion on which a diverse group is gathered for some common purpose.

My own opinion is that in such a situation Christ would not want me to insist on ending my prayer in Christ's name. I think Christ would want me to act with love and respect for those who are present. That behavior is the clearest witness I can give to my Christianity. The prayer should reflect the unity that we do have as fellow believers in a loving God. The prayer should be one to which all participants can say, "Amen."

BROTHER DOG (SEE CHAPTER 5)

Unlike St. Francis, I have not had a deep sense of, and apprecia-tion for, God's presence in all of creation. I am definitely a learner and not a teacher when it comes to this topic. However, there is no doubt that Scripture would have us stand in awe of all creation.

The very first story in the Bible, the story of God creating the world in six days (Gen 1:1–2:4), affirms over and over the good-ness of all creation. In fact, the sentence, "God saw how good it was" becomes a refrain in the story. As we mentioned in chapter 7, this story dates to the time after the Babylonian exile (587–537 B.C.), after the Israelites had been exposed to the beliefs of the Babylonians. The Babylonian story of creation, *Enuma Elish*, re-flects a dualism in their view of the world: they considered spirit good, but not matter. In the Israelite creation story, God looks at all that God has created, including the material things, and finds them "very good" (Gen 1:31).

Psalm 104 praises God not only for all that God has created, but for God's ongoing care of that creation:

> You send forth springs into the watercourses
> that wind among the mountains,
> And give drink to every beast of the field,
> till the wild asses quench their thirst.
> Beside them the birds of heaven dwell;
> from among the branches they send forth their song.
> You water the mountains from your palace,
> the earth is replete with the fruit of your works.
> You raise grass for the cattle,
> and vegetation for men's use. (Ps 104:10–14)

The author of Psalm 148 calls on all that God has created to praise God:

> Praise the Lord from the earth,
> you sea monsters and all depths;
> Fire and hail, snow and mist,
> storm winds that fulfill his word;
> You mountains and all you hills,
> you fruit trees and all you cedars;
> You wild beasts and all tame animals,
> you creeping things and you winged fowl. (Ps 148:7–10)

In addition to picturing God affirming the goodness of all of material creation, the first story of creation (Gen 1:1–2:4) shows God giving human beings authority over the rest of creation. After creating human beings in God's own image, God says, "Be fertile and multiply; fill the earth and subdue it. Have dominion over the fish of the sea, the birds of the air, and all the living things that move on the earth" (Gen 1:26–27).

The Gospel of John, in its opening hymn, pictures all that exists having been created by God's Word, a Word that becomes flesh and dwells among us (see chapter 7). The author of John, through Jesus's I AM statements, has Jesus identify himself with Yahweh and with elements of God's creation that are essential for life: light and bread. We are taught to discern God's creative Word in all that exists and to become one with that Word through receiving the bread of life.

Given all this, one place in which I am trying harder to discern Christ's presence is in all that the Word of God has called into being. I think we must exercise the "dominion" that human beings have been given over nature as God exercises God's dominion. After all, in the same story from Genesis, we are taught that we all, male and female, are created in God's own image. We must exercise our dominion over the rest of creation with love so that all of creation can flourish. We must regard environmental issues as moral issues. We must not diminish the evidence of God's glory as it is revealed in creation by abusing the gifts we have received.

As a Catholic, I am very used to blessing things: We bless animals. We bless homes. We bless oils. We bless water. After we bless the water, we call it *holy water.* As we enter church, we dip our finger into holy water and make the sign of the cross to remind ourselves of our first entrance into the Church, our baptism.

When I was younger, I thought that the blessing was making the water holy. I now think that the blessing is reminding us that what we take for granted is already truly holy. God made all that exists. Every drink of water that we have is a gift from a loving God. As we drink that water, we might hear a voice say, "I don't think you recognized me."

EUCHARIST: AN ESCHATOLOGICAL BANQUET

In chapter 4 we discussed Paul's account of Eucharist in 1 Corinthians and Paul's keen understanding that those who receive the body of Christ become the body of Christ. When we say that the risen Christ is truly present in Eucharist, we are already acknowledging that Eucharist is a meal that steps outside of time and space. Otherwise, the risen Christ could not be present.

As a Catholic, I am very accustomed to thinking of others who no longer live on earth as celebrating with us. In the Eucharistic prayer we remember that we are celebrating with Mary, Joseph, the apostles, and all the saints. The Eucharistic meal is celebrated not only by those of us on earth, but by those who have preceded us in following Christ through death to new life.

I once heard a priest express this profound insight in very simple and comforting language. The occasion was a funeral, one of the most painful funerals imaginable because a teenage boy had committed suicide. His parents, family, and friends were in an agony of loss and separation, not to mention anger. The priest wanted to help them discern Christ's presence, not only in Eucharist but in the gathered community and in the Word proclaimed. He also wanted them to realize that their son was not dead. He was still alive and embraced by God's love. So, he began his homily by saying, "Christ never comes late to mass, and he never comes alone."

This priest was doing for the young boy's family and for all present in the church what I have been trying to do in my own life ever since my father's death. He was helping those present to discern the presence of the risen Christ. In case any of those present had missed recognizing Christ's presence and redeeming love in the community that had gathered in Christ's name, in the passages from Scripture that were proclaimed, or in the Eucharist, the homilist was reminding them of these profound truths. In case any of them had temporarily forgotten their hope in resurrection, he was reminding them of that, too.

Death cannot separate us from our loved ones. We not only express, but can experience our unity in love with those who are no longer living on earth when we share with them the bread of heaven. How ironic it is that I now think of my father as sharing in the heavenly banquet, being united with all of us at Eucharist, when I never once shared Eucharist with him on earth. The divisions we unfortunately practice on earth have no place in the kingdom of God.

THE KINGDOM OF GOD

We use the word *heaven* to refer to the place or state of those who have passed through death and have risen with Christ into new life. Certainly the book of Revelation uses the word in that sense when it refers to the *heavenly court*, the setting from which all the action in the book proceeds (see chapter 6). In the book of Revelation, *heaven* is a place of no suffering, a place where the final victory of good over evil has been won.

However, the word *heaven*, in Scripture, is not always referring to such an otherworldly place. In Matthew's gospel, when we read Jesus's preaching about the *kingdom of heaven*, the phrase is synonymous not with an otherworldly *heaven*, but with the *kingdom of God*, the phrase that appears in parallel passages in Mark and Luke's Gospels. (Remember, Mark was a source for Matthew and Luke.) Matthew changes Mark's the *kingdom of God*, to the *kingdom of heaven*, not to change the meaning, but to be sensitive to his Jewish audience who considers God too holy to name.

The kingdom of God (the kingdom of *heaven* in Matthew) was the central topic of Jesus's preaching. Many of Jesus's parables were about the kingdom of God, beginning, "The kingdom of God is like. . . ." This kingdom is not one that we enter at death. We could be living in the kingdom of God both in this life and the next. This truth is evident from the Lord's Prayer, which Jesus taught his disciples. Jesus says,

> This is how you are to pray:
> Our Father in heaven,
> hallowed be your name,
> your kingdom come,
> your will be done,
> on earth as in heaven. (Matt 6:9–10)

"Your kingdom come" and "your will be done" are an example of parallel structure, a literary device common in Hebrew poetry. The second line repeats the thought of the first, only in different words. The two phrases are saying the same thing: God's kingdom reigns where God's will is done. To enter the kingdom we need not die physically. We need convert: turn away from sin and live according to God's revealed moral order.

When Paul talks about dying and rising with Christ, Paul is not always talking about physically dying and rising after death. Paul is also talking about dying to sin through baptism and rising from the baptismal waters to new life on earth. Paul says,

> Or are you unaware that we who were baptized into Christ Jesus were baptized into his death? We were indeed buried with him through baptism into death, so that, just as Christ was raised from the dead by the glory of the Father, we too might live in newness of life. . . . If then we have died with Christ, we believe that we shall also live with him. . . . Consequently, you, too, must think of yourselves as [being] dead to sin and living for God in Christ Jesus. (Rom 6:3–4, 8, 11)

So, for Paul, the major *dying* was not leaving earth, but dying to sin and living for Christ. Life after life on earth is a continuation of living in the kingdom of God, not the major transition. Certainly, Paul expects his life in Christ to continue when he leaves earth. He tells the Philippians, "For to me life is Christ, and death is gain. If I go on living in the flesh, that means fruitful labor for me. . . . I long to depart this life and be with Christ, [for] that is far better. Yet that I remain [in] the flesh is more necessary for your benefit" (Phil 1:21–22a, 23b–24).

So, the goal is that we live in the kingdom of God while on earth, freed from slavery to sin and growing in love. The more we love, the easier the transition to life after life on earth will be.

WE ARE NEVER ALONE; WE ARE ALWAYS LOVED

The core revelation of both the Old and New Testaments is that we are never alone and that we are always loved. If only we could believe that, all of life, especially our times of suffering, would be so much less difficult. From the very first story in Genesis, in which male and female are created by God in love, to the very last book in the Bible, the book of Revelation, in which the final victory over sin and death is celebrated, we are assured of God's presence and love. So many passages of Scripture assure us of God's presence and consolation, in both the Old and New Testaments: Isaiah says:

> Fear not, I am with you;
> be not dismayed; I am your God.
> I will strengthen you and help you,
> and uphold you with my right hand of justice. (Is 41:10)

Proverbs advises us:

> Trust in the Lord with all your heart,
> on your own intelligence rely not;
> In all your ways be mindful of him,
> and he will make straight your paths. (Prov 3:5–6)

In John, Jesus assures us: "Peace I leave with you; my peace I give to you. Not as the world gives do I give it to you. Do not let your hearts be troubled or afraid" (John 14:27).

Despite these comforting words, we sometimes do let our hearts become troubled and afraid. Sometimes, when our loved ones die, we are in sorrow not only because we will miss their presence but because we know of their faults, their infidelities, and we worry about their final destiny. Where is Christ in a situation like this?

Three truths remain firm. The first is that God loves this person even more than we do. The second is that our love and prayers can still be present for that person. We can pray for him or her, and prayer is powerful. The third is that God is always ready to forgive. Jesus was revealing God's constant offer of forgiveness when he forgave those who were crucifying him, right at the time that the crucifixion was taking place.

So, once more, our hope rests in the revelation we have received through Jesus Christ, his cross, and his resurrection. When it comes right down to it, death is not death. Our bond of love remains. Through prayer, we place our departed loved ones in God's loving hands, never despairing because we know that "all things are possible with God" (Matt 19:26).

SPIRITUAL LESSONS LEARNED/ REFLECTIONS

1. One cannot love and avoid suffering.

   - How has suffering been integral to loving in my life?
   - In what ways has this suffering been transformative for me or for others?
   - How has suffering "perfected" me, helped me grow?

   "When Jesus saw [Mary] weeping and the Jews who had come with her weeping, he became perturbed and deeply troubled, and said, 'Where have you laid him?' They said to him, 'Sir, come and see.' And Jesus wept. So the Jews said, 'See how he loved him'" (John 11:33–36).

2. The beliefs that Christ rose from the dead and that my loved ones have life after death go hand in hand.

   - Do I truly believe that Christ rose from the dead? Why?
   - Do I truly believe that my loved ones have life after death? Why?
   - Does this belief give me comfort?

   "God raised the Lord and will also raise us by his power" (1 Cor 6:14).

3. If we love people we must give them the freedom to become the people God is calling them to be.

   - Do I leave my loved ones free to become who God is calling them to be?

- Do I give myself that same freedom?

"Thus says the Lord, who created you . . . / Fear not, for I have redeemed you; / I have called you by name: you are mine" (Is 43:1).

4. For the unity that God desires for all of God's children to occur, we must learn to forgive and to love.

- Do I believe that the human race is called to be one?
- What prejudices will I have to overcome in order to cooperate with this call?
- Why is forgiveness a necessary component of being one?

"Then Peter approaching asked him, 'Lord, if my brother sins against me, how often must I forgive him? As many as seven times?' Jesus answered, 'I say to you, not seven times but seventy-seven times'" (Matt 18:21–22).

5. Human beings have been given authority over all of creation.

- What moral obligations are integral to having authority over creation?
- What behaviors do I practice that reflect thoughtless consumerism rather than care for God's creation?

"God blessed them, saying: 'Be fertile and multiply; fill the earth and subdue it. Have dominion over the fish of the sea, the birds of the air, and all the living things that move on the earth'" (Gen 1:28).

6. Eucharist is an eschatological meal that joins heaven and earth.

- Do I believe that Christ is present in Eucharist?

- Do I believe that members of the body of Christ who have risen with Christ can be present celebrating with those of us who are still on earth?

"And it happened that, while he was with them at table, he took bread, said the blessing, broke it, and gave it to them. With that their eyes were opened and they recognized him, but he vanished from their sight" (Luke 24:30–31).

7. God's kingdom is both on earth and in heaven.

- Am I living in the kingdom of God? If not, what conversion on my part is necessary?
- What divisions are there here on earth that have no place in the kingdom of God?
- What can I do to heal some of these divisions?

"Repent, for the kingdom of heaven is at hand" (Matt 3:2). "The kingdom of God is among you" (Luke 17:21).

8. We are always loved. We are never alone.

- Do I believe in God's love and God's caring presence both for me and my loved ones?
- Do I believe that all things are possible with God?
- What can I do to actually live in the peace that Christ wants to give me?

"I will not leave you orphans. I will come to you" (John 14:18).

APPENDIX 1: CONTEXTS TO CONSIDER WHEN READING SCRIPTURE

It may well be that the reader has never had an opportunity to learn how to understand Scripture as a *contextualist,* as a person who considers context. Therefore, it seems wise to offer a more detailed explanation of this approach to interpreting Scripture than I do in the Introduction for those who are encountering this method of interpretation for the first time.

A contextualist's interpretation of Scripture is in contrast to a fundamentalist's. The difference is not in whether or not one believes that biblical authors are inspired and that Scripture contains revelation. Both contextualists and fundamentalists believe that. The difference is not about whether Scripture has authority in one's life or not. For both contextualists and fundamentalists, Scripture has authority. The difference is in how one goes about understanding what the inspired biblical authors are teaching, in how one understands the truths being taught. In short: A fundamentalist attributes meaning to biblical passages without considering context. A contextualist considers context in order to determine meaning.

There are three contexts that contextualists consider: literary form (What kind of writing are we reading?), the presumed and shared beliefs of the author and audience, and the fact that Scripture contains a two-thousand-year process of coming to knowledge about mysteries that to some extent are still beyond our comprehension. We will explain each of these contexts, applying them to passages that are relevant to the overall topic of this book: the death of a parent, the suffering such a loss involves, and the spiritual and biblical lessons learned from such an experience.

THE CONTEXT OF LITERARY FORM

The Bible is a library of books, not a book with chapters. The books in the Bible are written in many different literary forms. If we misunderstand the kind of writing we are reading, we will misunderstand the intent of the author and, therefore, the truth that God intends to reveal to God's people through the inspired author's writing.

We all have the ability to distinguish one kind of writing from another, even if we do not know the names of the different literary forms and literary devices. For instance, when an author pictures an animal or plant talking just as though it were a human being, we know that we are not reading history. We may or may not know that this literary device is called *personification*. Nevertheless, we realize that we are not reading an eyewitness account of an event. Rather, we are reading a story composed by an author to teach a lesson.

For example, we know that the story many of us read as children that describes a conversation between a tortoise and a hare is not teaching history and claiming a miracle. Rather, it is teaching the value of perseverance through a literary form that we call *fable*. What the story is teaching is true. However, the author teaches this truth, learned from experience, by composing an imaginative story, not by describing an experience.

Any literary form can be a vehicle for truth, and any literary form can fail to be a vehicle for truth. Because the Bible contains many different literary forms (myths, legends, genealogies, etiologies, birth narratives, parables, allegories, etc.), we need to bring this ability to distinguish one kind of writing from another, which we use routinely in our everyday lives, to our reading of the Bible.

To apply this insight to the Bible and to the topic at hand, let us turn to the story of the man and woman in the garden (Gen 2:4–3:24). This story uses personification. One of the main characters in the story is a serpent that carries on a conversation with Eve, just as though the serpent were a human being. The story also includes many obvious symbols, such as a tree of life and a tree of knowledge of good and evil. By using these literary devices, the author has informed us that the story is not teaching history. However, that does not at all mean that the story is not teaching truth. As we discuss in chapter 6, this story is teaching something true about suffering. The truth that the inspired author is teaching is that sin inevitably causes suffering.

In order to understand a book's literary form and the truth that the inspired author is teaching through that form, we must read the whole story or book. If we simply take a sentence or two out of the middle of a book, and ascribe meaning to those out-of-context sentences, we have no way of knowing whether or not the meaning we are attributing to the words has anything to do with what the inspired author uses the words to say. Therefore, it is absolutely essential that we read a whole biblical book and determine the literary form of that book in order to understand the meaning of any biblical passage.

THE CONTEXT OF THE BELIEFS OF THE TIME

The second context that we must consider in order to understand the meaning of any biblical passage is the beliefs and presumptions that are shared by the original author and audience. In the process of teaching universal truths, biblical authors use examples or make applications that reflect presumptions of the time, pre-sumptions that later generations do not share. We do not put the authority of Scripture behind an author's presumptions or applica-tions. We put the authority of Scripture behind the core truth that the author is teaching.

We can illustrate this point by turning to the very first story in the Bible, the story of the creation of the world in six days. We discuss some of what this story is teaching in chapters 7 and 8: that God created all that exists, that human beings, both male and female, are created in God's image, and that what God has created is very good. These are eternal truths that are at the basis of many of our social justice teachings.

However, the author also names some presumptions of his time, presumptions that our scientific age does not share. For instance, the author presumes that the earth is flat and has a dome over it. That is why the author pictures God separating the waters above the dome from the waters beneath the dome.

The author of Job also presumes that the earth is flat and rests upon posts. That is why he pictures God asking Job: "Where were you when I founded the earth? / . . . Who determined its size; do you know? / Who stretched out the measuring line for it? / Into what were its pedestals sunk?" (Job 38:4, 5–6). However, the au-thor is not trying to teach the shape of the earth. Rather, the author is teaching, through the literary form *debate*, that not all suffering is punishment for sin.

Since inspired biblical authors, in the course of teaching uni-versal truths, include presumptions of their time, presumptions they are not teaching, a contextualist must determine an author's intent and put the authority of Scripture behind the truth being taught, not behind the presumptions of the time. That truth will always have something to say about our relationship with God and with each other, about how we are to act lovingly so as to live in right relationship. It will be a spiritual truth, such as, "Every hu-man being is of great dignity," not a scientific truth, such as, "The earth is round."

THE CONTEXT OF A PROCESS OF REVELATION

The third context that we must consider in order to determine what an inspired author is teaching is the context of a process of revelation. This means that we must consider the truth that the author is teaching in the context of the two-thousand-year process of coming to knowledge that the Bible models. We discuss several examples of this context in this book: the process of coming to knowledge about life after death, about the ramifications of the fact that God is love, and about the purposes of suffering.

To illustrate the importance of considering this context, I will use as an example the process of understanding the purposes of suffering that appears in the Bible. In fact, we have already laid the foundation for this topic while discussing the contexts of literary form and of the presumptions of the time.

As we have said, the story of the man and woman in the garden teaches that sin causes suffering. This story dates to about 1000 B.C. It teaches something universally true: Sin does cause suffering because it changes who we are: It changes our ability to be in right relationship with God, self, others, and our earth. When we sin we bring suffering on ourselves and others.

For hundreds of years, people believed not only that sin causes suffering, but that all suffering is due to sin. In other words, people took a partial truth and understood it as the whole truth, thus ending up in error. The author of Job was courageous enough to argue against this belief of his time. He did not think that all suffering was due to sin. So, he wrote a debate in which Job's friends, Eliphaz, Bildad, Zophar, and Elihu argue the belief of the time: All suffering is due to sin. Then the author has God come on stage and say that the friends are wrong.

This inspired author added to our understanding by teaching that suffering has a purpose other than punishment for sin. However, he lived in the sixth century, before the Israelites had come to a belief in life after death. Therefore, he could not probe the mystery of innocent suffering with as much insight as could those authors who lived after Jesus's suffering, death, and resurrection.

The Gospels and the letters give us even more insight into the topic of suffering.

If a person neglects to consider this third context, that person is vulnerable to misinterpreting the Bible by taking an early insight and treating it as though that insight represents the fullness of revelation. People do this when they teach an eye for an eye and a tooth for a tooth (see Ex 21:24; the Exodus took place around 1250 B.C.). They are completely ignoring Jesus's admonition: "You have heard that it was said, 'An eye for an eye and a tooth for a tooth.' But I say to you, offer no resistance to one who is evil . . ." (Matt 5:38–39). To ignore this process of revelation is once more to misunderstand, and perhaps misrepresent, what the Bible actually teaches.

Before we draw conclusions about what the Bible actually teaches, it is extremely important that those of us who believe that Scripture is inspired and teaches eternal truths do our best to understand biblical passages in the contexts of the literary form in which they appear, the beliefs of the time of the author and audience, and the two-thousand-year process of revelation that the Bible contains. Otherwise we are in danger of putting the authority of Scripture behind our own prejudices and misunderstandings rather than behind God's self-revelation to God's beloved people.

APPENDIX 2: SCRIPTURE AS A LIVING WORD

In Appendix 1, I claimed that in order to understand the universal truths that inspired biblical authors are teaching we must understand their words in context. While this is true, it is also true that out-of-context biblical passages can speak directly to people's hearts, correcting them, encouraging them, and enlightening them. Are these two claims compatible with each other? If so, how?

Years ago, when I, as an English major, first learned to be a biblical contextualist and to consider literary form, I became very suspicious of people who simply "cracked open" the Bible and claimed that the Bible taught whatever meaning they attached to the words. I regarded this as a form of self-delusion, as a way of having God affirm whatever the person already thought and wanted to keep thinking. In fact, I wrote an article explaining why cracking open the Bible was not a way to discern God's will in one's life.

I sent the article to a teacher of mine, the same teacher I mention in chapter 1, who encouraged me to write. He wrote back that he thought the article was very well written. The only problem was that I was wrong. Scripture is a living word, and many, many people have experienced it as such. He gave me two famous examples. When St. Augustine was trying to decide whether or not to become a Christian, thus giving up his mistress, he opened the New Testament and read: "Put on the Lord Jesus Christ, and make no provision for the desires of the flesh" (Rom 13:14). Augustine heard these words as God speaking directly to him in response to his dilemma, and he did just that.

When Thomas Merton was trying to decide whether or not to enter Gethsemane, a monastery where the monks practice periods of silence, he opened the New Testament and read the angel Gabriel's words to John the Baptist's father that he would not be able to speak: "But now you will be speechless and unable to talk" (Luke 1:20). Merton, too, heard these words as God speaking to him, and he entered Gethsemane.

My teacher told me that while these were examples from famous people, many, many people have experienced the same thing. They will be reading Scripture while ruminating over some personal problem or dilemma, and certain words just seem to jump off the page and speak to them personally. My teacher believed that the author of Hebrews was absolutely correct when he said, "Indeed, the word of God is living and effective . . . and able to discern reflections and thoughts of the heart" (Heb 4:12).

Sometime after this I had the same experience myself. A close friend had done something that hurt me, and I was feeling "sinned against." That is the phrase that was in my mind. I didn't open Scripture to find an answer. I opened Scripture to prepare a class I was teaching. However, the words that jumped off the page were, "Who are you to pass judgment on someone else's servant?" (Rom 14:4). For some reason that I cannot explain, those words stuck with me. By feeling "sinned against" I was judging the servant of another. My friend was responsible to God, not to me. Perhaps my friend had a reason for acting as she did. Why was I acting as if the whole situation revolved around me and that I knew all the circumstances? The more those words sunk in, the more my hurt disappeared.

In the examples my teacher gave me from Augustine's and Merton's lives, Scripture as a living word gave guidance. In the example from my own life, Scripture as a living word offered correction. Every time I have had this experience, Scripture has corrected me. It has never once told me what was wrong with someone else.

Once I was convinced that Scripture can be a living word I began to notice that Jesus used it that way, too. For instance, when Jesus is preaching in the synagogue in Nazareth he reads from the scroll of Isaiah:

> The Spirit of the Lord is upon me,
> because he has anointed me
> to bring glad tidings to the poor.
> He has sent me to proclaim liberty to captives
> and recovery of sight to the blind,
> to let the oppressed go free,
> and to proclaim a year acceptable to the Lord. (Luke 4:18–19)

Jesus heard Isaiah's call story as directed at himself, as describing his role and ministry. That is why he tells the people, "Today this Scripture passage is fulfilled in your hearing" (Luke 4:21).

In fact, as we discuss in chapter 4, the Church understands Scripture as a living word when, during Advent, we proclaim Isaiah's messianic prophesies and understand them to be speaking about Jesus. We do the same thing when, in Holy Week, we proclaim 2 Isaiah's suffering servant songs and understand them to be speaking about Jesus. That is why, when Matthew quotes Isaiah's words in reference to Jesus, he says, "All this took place to fulfill what the Lord had said through the prophet" (Matt 1:22). The prophets' words had deeper meanings than even they understood. Although we do not claim that the original prophet intended to say what we now take the words to mean, we do accept the deeper meaning and attribute that meaning to God.

So, I became convinced of two truths: In order to understand what an inspired biblical author is teaching we must put the author's words in the context in which they appear in the Bible. At the same time, Scripture is a living word, both in individual people's lives and for the Church as a whole. The original author's intent does not exhaust the meaning of the words.

How are these two truths compatible with each other? If Scripture is a living word, why is it important to be a contextualist?

If one acknowledges that Scripture is a living word, it is all the more important to be a contextualist. Why? Because Scripture as a living word cannot contradict the eternal truths that we learn from understanding the intent of the inspired authors. As a living word, a passage of Scripture can be understood in a different setting to address a different question than the author was addressing, but this additional meaning cannot contradict the basic spiritual truths taught by the inspired authors.

In other words, Scripture is a living word, but when we hear Scripture as a living word we are hearing personal guidance, not universal truths that are equally applicable to every situation. What St. Augustine and Thomas Merton heard was certainly personal guidance. Not everyone is called to become a priest or a monk. So, when we hear Scripture as a living word we cannot claim that the Bible teaches what we took the words to mean. We can only claim that these living words spoke to us personally in a way that we experienced as spiritually helpful, as a light on our paths.

To understand Scripture as a living word, but not understand the core spiritual messages of Scripture, can be very dangerous, as history attests. Over the course of history many people have used Scripture as a living word to justify their own prejudices and misunderstandings or to manipulate others for their own purposes. They claim that Scripture supports what Scripture does not support. An example will make this point clear.

Say a person has a prejudice against anyone who has AIDS. This person regards having AIDS in the same way people regarded leprosy in the New Testament. For the good of society such people should be marginalized. There is no need to reach out to them or help them because they deserve what is happening to them. God punishes sinners. To prove the point this person quotes the book of Job:

As I see it, those who plow for mischief
and sow trouble, reap the same.
By the breath of God they perish,
and by the blast of his wrath they are consumed. (Job 4:8–9)

On the basis of this passage from Scripture, the person feels justified in judging and condemning another human being, confident that God agrees.

A contextualist would not make this mistake. A contextualist would consider literary form, read the whole book of Job, know that it is a debate, and realize that the words quoted are on the lips of Eliphaz, whom God later declares to be wrong (see Job 42:7).

A contextualist would consider the beliefs of the time and the process of revelation, and realize that the presumption that the suffering observed must be deserved was a belief in the sixth century B.C., but the author is arguing against that belief.

A contextualist would be open to Jesus's message that we must love each other, especially the marginalized. Why? Because every person is a beloved child of God, and the way we are treating that person is the way we are treating the risen Christ.

There are examples of people misusing Scripture as a living word within Scripture itself. In a number of Jesus's encounters, his adversaries use Scripture as a living word to come to false conclusions or to manipulate others. In argument after argument, the Pharisees use Scripture to justify their opposition to Jesus (see Matt 12:2). Satan, too, quotes Scripture as he tempts Jesus to abuse his power (see Matt 4:1–11). Just because a person quotes Scripture does not mean that the person is right.

It is wonderful to hear Scripture as a living word. Scripture is meant to be a light upon our paths. However, if we do make choices and decisions based on hearing Scripture as a living word, it is essential that we are also contextualists. Otherwise we might use out-of-context passages to justify behavior that directly contradicts what the inspired biblical authors are teaching.

BIBLIOGRAPHY

Books to Give Comfort to Those in Grief and to Help Loved Ones Offer Comfort to Those in Grief

The following books have been recommended as helpful by chaplains and hospice workers for those who are in grief as well as for those who are accompanying people in grief.

Albom, Mitch. *Tuesdays with Morrie: An Old Man, a Young Man, and Life's Greatest Lessons.* New York: Broadway Books, 2002.

Byock, Ira. *The Four Things That Matter Most: A Book About Living.* New York: Free Press, 2004.

———. *Dying Well: Peace and Possibilities at the End of Life.* New York: Riverhead Books, 1997.

Callahan, Maggie, and Patricia Kelley. *Final Gifts: Understanding the Special Awareness, Needs, and Communications of the Dying.* New York: Simon and Schuster Paperbacks, 1992.

Colgrove, Melba, Harold H. Bloomfield, and Peter McWilliams. *How to Survive the Loss of a Love.* Los Angeles: Prelude Press, 1991.

Davis, Nancy D., Ellen Cole, and Esther C. Rothblum, eds. *Faces of Women and Aging.* New York: The Haworth Press, 1993.

Farley, Margaret A. *Compassionate Respect: A Feminist Approach to Medical Ethics and Other Questions.* Mahwah, NJ: Paulist Press, 2002.

Kübler-Ross, Elisabeth. *On Death and Dying.* New York: Scribner, 1969.

———. *Living with Death and Dying.* New York: Touchstone, 1981.

Kushner, Harold S. *When Bad Things Happen to Good People.* New York: Anchor Books, 1981.

———. *The Lord Is My Shepherd.* New York: Random House, 2003.

Lester, Andrew D., and Judith L. Lester. *Understanding Aging Parents.* Louisville, KY: Westminster John Knox Publishers, 1980.

Lucado, Max. *Safe in the Shepherd's Arms.* Nashville, TN: J. Countryman, 2002.

Marshall, Fiona. *Losing a Parent: Practical Help for You and Other Family Members.* Tucson, AZ: Fisher Books, 2009.

Myers, Edward. *When a Parent Dies: A Guide for Adults.* New York: Penguin Books, 1997.

Willig, Rev. Jim, and Tammy Bundy. *Lessons from the School of Suffering.* Cincinnati, OH: St. Anthony Messenger Press, 2001.

BIBLICAL INDEX

ABOUT THE AUTHOR

Margaret Nutting Ralph is the director of the Masters in Pastoral Studies program at Lexington Theological Seminary. She has published many books, including *Why the Catholic Church Must Change: A Necessary Conversation*, *A Walk Through the New Testament: An Introduction for Catholics* and *And God Said What? An Introduction to Biblical Literary Forms*.